THE WORD & THE WAY

by Donald M. M

Illustrations by
Eric Aldwinckle and
Willis S. Wheatley

THE UNITED CHURCH PUBLISHING HOUSE
TORONTO   CANADA

Donald M. Mathers is professor of systematic theology at Queen's
Theological College, Kingston, Ontario ● Eric Aldwinckle is a
well-known Canadian artist ● Willis S. Wheatley is art director
of the Department of Sunday School Publications of The United
Church ● Norman McNairn is editor of adult publications, Department of Sunday School Publications, and author of the STUDY GUIDE
accompanying this book ● Peter Gordon White is editor-in-chief,
Department of Sunday School Publications.

First Printing, March, 1962 — 50,000
Second Printing, August, 1962 — 50,000

Contents

PART THREE: The Church and the World

*A glossary and index will be found
in the* STUDY GUIDE, *which is a com-
panion to this book, containing aids
for personal, family, and group study.*

Introduction

THIS book is for men and women who need a mature faith to meet the demands of their adult life. It was written as a result of one of those accidental discoveries about which one should say reverently, "Thank God we found out."

A few years ago a number of hearings were held across Canada to determine what was desirable in a New Curriculum for Sunday church schools. To the dismay of the survey team, many of the people consulted said in effect, Why ask us, what do we know about it?

The question was disturbing. Was the church asking its members to teach Christianity before discovering its meaning for their own lives? It was also humbling. Is the church expecting people to live a faith about which they know almost nothing? Do lay people leave the gospel to ministers and other professional church workers? Is the Bible really a closed book? Do we join a church only for companionship and prestige? Three questions seemed to sum up all the others:

First, how can we know God today, hear his word, and respond to his claims?

Second, who is Jesus Christ and what is the meaning of his life for us?

Third, what is the church and what does it mean to belong to this community?

Obviously these are adult questions. Some of the answers may be disturbing, and when first heard may only raise more questions. For this reason it will be good if THE WORD AND THE WAY can be discussed with friends and neighbours. Independent thinking will be sharpened and strengthened as individuals meet each other face-to-face, open and receptive to the leading of the Holy Spirit.

For this is the fundamental conviction of the book: the Spirit of God is active among us, seeking us out where we are, calling us to be children of God now. To be aware of this is life. Anything less is unreality.

To meet and discuss such matters is richly rewarding, but not easy when first attempted. To overcome some of these difficulties, a STUDY GUIDE booklet is available. It gives the practical advice needed for starting a group and continuing it successfully. Bible passages, glossary, questions for discussion, summaries and other helps are included.

So it has come about that a book for every adult member of the church takes precedence over other materials of the New Curriculum. THE WORD AND THE WAY is a basic book, a summary of fundamental Christian convictions. It will be followed by other resources for adult reading and study.

This is a modest beginning for a large undertaking. But for people who find a source of new spiritual vitality in this experience, it could be one of those significant "beginnings" that some call hope, and others joy.

Peter Gordon White

UNITED CHURCH HOUSE
1962

PART ONE

God and His Purpose

Chapter 1

What Is Religion?

*Religion continues to be man's vital
concern. Some religions are an escape
from life's hard facts. Others seek
what man wants. This is idolatry. The
highest and truest religion responds
to God and seeks what he wants.*

For a hundred years the critics of religion
have been telling us that it is on the way out. Religion,
they say, belongs to the age of witch doctors and savage
rituals. Like them it should be replaced by science,
education and enlightenment.

The French thinker Comte said there were three
ages in human history, the age of religious superstition,
the age of philosophy, and the age of science, in which
reason would finally hold sway. In the 1840's he believed the age of science was finally dawning, and
religion could soon be expected to disappear.

Karl Marx, the founder of communism, wrote that
religion was the "opium of the people," and the oppres-

sive capitalist class was using it to keep the workers in subjection and fear. Once communist democracy arrived, predicted Marx, religion would wither away like the other evils of a dark age.

1. RELIGION IS AS ALIVE AS EVER

Still Christianity survives both its own perversions and the attacks of its enemies. In the last hundred years the church has grown faster than at any other time in its history. It has spread out into Asia and Africa to become a world church, not only in name, but also in fact. Its vitality has been shown by its ability, not only to survive, but to reform itself and to adapt itself to new conditions.

And not only Christianity survives. Other ancient religions, Hinduism, Buddhism, and Islam, are showing new signs of life. Far from being on the way out, religion seems to be as alive and powerful as ever.

Even more startling, secular movements like communism, take on the appearance of new religions. Communism has

its holy scriptures (*The Communist Manifesto* and *Das Kapital*);

its prophets (Marx, who predicted the revolution);

its saints (Lenin, whose relics in Moscow's Red Square are like a mediaeval shrine, visited daily by troops of pilgrims);

its church (the Communist Party) with its headquarters in Moscow ("the third Rome");

its heretics (Trotsky);

its reformers (Tito).

This all goes to show that when people try to abolish religion they usually succeed only in exchanging a good one for a bad imitation.

So religion continues to be a human concern. "There has never been a country or family, from the beginning of the world," wrote Calvin, "totally destitute of religion." We have learned a great deal since Calvin's time about human history and human behaviour. It has only confirmed his statement. Those who are glad of this say it proves that God never leaves himself without a witness. Those who regret it say that man is incurably religious. Good or bad, the fact is there: *religion seems to be a permanent and universal part of human life.* If we have a choice, it is not between having a religion and not having one, but between having a genuine faith or an inferior substitute.

2. WHAT TURNS MEN TO RELIGION?

Since religion is a permanent and universal part of human life there must be some strong force that turns men towards it. After all, religion is not so obviously attractive. It is usually associated with serious thoughts, with strictness and self denial. What could ever make it popular? It sometimes leads people to suffering and martyrdom. Why should they choose it?

One famous answer is given in the story about the Buddha and the Four Passing Sights. The Buddha's father had been told that his son would become either the emperor of all India or a homeless monk. Having worldly ambitions for the boy he decided to isolate him from anything that might make him religious. He brought him up in a palace where he knew only young, healthy and happy people. One day the Buddha, having grown up, drove out on the roads and saw a sick man, an old man, a funeral, and a monk in a yellow robe. Learning what disease, age, and death meant, he was so shocked at the discovery of the futile and tragic aspect of life that he went off to be a monk himself and to seek his own salvation.

There we see one answer to the question, "What turns men to religion?" When men feel that life in this world is meaningless, and search for a salvation beyond it they are turning to religion. This leads to a gloomy kind of religion: a religion of escape from a world that seems hopeless. There is much in Buddhism that we can admire and agree with, but there are real differences between it and Christianity, and one of them is this:

> Buddhism teaches that religion begins when men realize the futility of earthly life and turn away from it to seek their own salvation.

> The Christian, indeed the biblical teaching, is that true religion begins when God speaks and men hear.

If you compare the story of the Buddha with that of Moses you find a very different answer to the question of what turns men to religion. Like the Buddha, Moses was brought up in luxury, protected from the hardships of life in the palace of Pharaoh. When he left Pharaoh's palace, however, it was not because he was renouncing the world to seek salvation. It was because he had killed an Egyptian for abusing a Hebrew slave. It all seems a much less religious story than that of Buddha's great renunciation. And so it continues:

Buddha becomes a wandering monk, a holy man and
a religious teacher.

Moses becomes a shepherd, marries and rears a
family.

Buddha, after years of prayer and meditation
achieves enlightenment, escapes the bonds of desire,
and enters into oneness with reality.

Moses, while working as a shepherd, is con-
fronted by God in a burning bush, and is sent
back to Egypt to lead his people out of bondage.

Buddha encounters no god. He achieves salvation
for himself. He makes no claim to a divine revelation, but he does make a claim of personal holiness.

Moses makes no claim to personal virtue (and
the Bible is very frank about his personal weaknesses); indeed he protests that he is unworthy
to serve God. But he does claim that God has
spoken to him, chosen him for a special task,
and sent him out to do it.

Buddha for the rest of his life was a religious teacher,
secluded from worldly affairs, showing others how
to attain the serenity and enlightenment he had
reached.

Moses, for the rest of his life, was an active leader
of the tribes of Israel, a lawgiver, a soldier, and
a judge. He did not seek to make others like
himself, but he did claim to be speaking in God's
name.

Buddha claimed to be able to teach individuals how
to work out their own salvation.

Moses claimed to be appointed by God to forge
a people into an instrument for God's purposes.

What turned Buddha to religion was his desire to escape from life's sorrow. Moses probably would have said that he did not turn to religion at all, but that God called him into service.

The contrast between Moses and the Buddha seems to point to a contrast between two types of religion. For the Buddha, what is important is that one should achieve salvation, and he claims to have found the way and to be able to teach it to others. If they follow his example they can save themselves. Buddha does not speak of God. Indeed he does not believe in God at all in the sense in which the people of the Bible do. He has a religious way of life to teach.

For Moses, everything begins and ends with God. Moses claims that God has made himself known. God speaks and commands. Man's part is to obey in order that God's will may be done. It seems that Moses does not think much about his own salvation. He hardly thinks about himself at all. He thinks rather about God and God's will. Since God is good and holy and righteous, he is to be obeyed and trusted.

For the Buddha, religion begins with man and his problems, and the religious life is the attempt to solve these problems and gain blessedness. For Moses, religion begins with God and his will, and the religious life is the attempt to do God's will and be faithful. Salvation is not something that we can get for ourselves, but God's gift.

3. RELIGION VERSUS GOD

If anyone had asked Moses whether he was starting a new religion, he probably wouldn't have known what they meant. If you think of religion as something people can start, or take up, or turn to, or be keen on, then Moses would have had a low opinion of it. There was plenty of that kind of thing in the ancient as in the modern world; cults of various sorts that men had started as ways to obtain the blessings that they wanted for themselves or their families or their nations.

Moses and the other great teachers of the Old Testament seem to have been strangely intolerant of such religion, calling it a worship of idols. To them the religion of Israel was not just another national cult to be set alongside the worship of Egypt or Canaan. Jehovah was not just another god like Amon of Thebes or Marduk of Babylon. Jehovah was the true and living God, not an idol. And the religion of Israel was not another human religion, but the response to the call of the true God. They believed that the great difference between their religion and others was that God was responsible for theirs, while men had invented the rest.

This is why, in the Old Testament, faith means something more than merely "being religious." It means hearing God and obeying him.

In the first of the ten commandments the Lord says:
*Thou shalt have no other gods before me . . . for I
the Lord thy God am a jealous God (Ex. 20:5).*

This has a harsh sound, for jealousy is not something we like in human beings. It might be objected that this makes God look like a universal bully, refusing to give the other gods fair play. But as you read the rest of the Old Testament its meaning becomes clear. The problem men face is not that of deciding which religion out of many they are to follow. Their problem is simply whether they are to worship the true God, the only God there is.

There are many religions, but there is only one God. The faith to which Moses was calling his people was not just one national religion among others, the religion of Israel as distinguished from the Egyptian or the Baby-lonian. It was the worship of the one true God. He was not calling on the Israelites to be more patriotic through loyalty to their own God. He was calling on them to give up the whole business of man-made political reli-gions and worship the true God.

4. THE STRUGGLE AGAINST IDOLATRY

This is the real meaning of the condemnation of idolatry. An idol is not just a graven image made of silver or gold and set up in a pagan temple to be wor-shipped. *Any earthly and finite thing which takes the place of God and claims the worship that is due to him alone is an idol.*

The Jews would not permit pictures or statues of God to be made. This did not spring from their being in-artistic or puritanical, opposed to religious ritual or ornament. It sprang from the desire to worship the true God only, and not any of the finite powers worshipped in pagan religions. Man-made images in pagan temples seemed to Israel to represent a worship of earthly things like political power or personal prosperity or happiness.

From this point of view there is real importance in the prohibition of idols. Religion in the ancient world was mostly idolatry. The worship of tribal gods or city gods or sacred kings was a way of harnessing religion to a political purpose, to make people obedient servants of the state. Magic was an attempt to make supernatural powers of various sorts serve men's purposes. Fertility cults like the worship of the Baals spoken of in the Old Testament (2 Kings 21) were ways of inducing the gods in charge of reproduction to make the cows calve or the crops grow or the wives of the worshippers bear many sons: all to increase human power and wealth.

It is not wrong to be patriotic or to desire wealth and success. But these should not be our first consideration in life. Our first consideration should be God and his will. To let anything else take the place of that is to be guilty of idolatry.

The temptation to idolatry is still a real one. Political religions are just as powerful as ever. Communism is an obvious example. The temptation to give to a party or a state or a movement that absolute devotion which belongs only to God is always with us.

Fertility religions are not entirely a thing of the past either. I do not mean simply that the strong emotions of religion and the strong emotions of sex still occasionally get intermingled. Fertility religion was never merely a matter of sex: it was concerned with wealth and with productivity. In the days before machines, productivity depended on human births. Wealth depended on the natural increase of crops and animals. It was to make the crops grow and the animals multiply that the strange rites of fertility religion were performed. Fertility religion is simply the worship of mammon.

Among Christian people there ought to be no counterpart of this. We all know that when we put our love of wealth and our concern for possessions before our love of God, and even try to use our religion to make us wealthy we are not acting so very differently from the ancient pagan who offered sacrifices to Aphrodite or the Baals, gods in charge of fertility.

Is not this one warning sign of *our* idolatry, that we sometimes make use of religion for our own purposes? Suppose a person goes to church not to worship God, but because at church he can make contacts that help him in his business. Or suppose someone practises religion, not because God ought to be worshipped and his will done, but because he has come to believe that religion makes people happy. Happiness or prosperity are being placed in this way on a higher level than God himself, and so are being made into idols. It may well be true that religious people have a better chance of being happy and prosperous than others, but they should not be religious for that reason. If they are, they will probably be disappointed.

When things go badly with us, what we do shows what is our real religion. We are all sinners, so we are probably all guilty of the worship of false gods to some extent. We will find out how far gone we are in idolatry when real trouble comes along. If we are tempted to say, "Well, that didn't work. I will try some other way of life"; then we know that we are not serving God for his own sake and have placed some idol higher than him. If we say, "Come fair, come foul, I must do the right," then we have some indication that our faith is real.

5. WHAT THEN IS REAL RELIGION?

We have looked at some of the main sources of religion. One was the desire to escape from the sorrow and tragedy of human life. Another was the attempt to harness the natural or supernatural forces of the world to obtain what we want. The third was a response to the call of God. To illustrate these sources of religion we used as examples the religion of the Buddha, idolatry in its various forms, and the religion of Moses.

Perhaps it would be true to say that for the average person all these different elements play some part in his religious quest. We turn to religion because apart from it our deepest needs are unsatisfied. And many truly spiritual people are glad to testify that religion meets the everyday needs as well. So we read in Psalms 103,

> Bless the Lord, O my soul,
>   and forget not all his benefits,
> who forgives all your iniquity,
>   who heals all your diseases . . .
> who satisfies you with good
>   as long as you live. . . .

Even the Christian gospel, which we regard as religion in its highest form, contains all three elements to some degree. Jesus taught his followers to pray, among other things, that they should be given their daily bread, and that they should be delivered from evil.

Nevertheless religion does not arrive at its highest unless and until it puts ahead of everything else the desire to love and serve God. One of the greatest expressions of this insight into the true nature of

religion is found in the words of the prophet Micah
(6:8):

> He has showed you, O man, what is good;
>   and what does the Lord require of you
> but to do justice, and to love kindness,
>   and to walk humbly with your God?

This is also the teaching of Jesus. It is precisely what
he meant when he said, "Instead, seek his kingdom,
and these things shall be yours as well" (Luke 12:31).

If the highest form of religion is rooted in the desire
to serve God, if it is a response to the call of God to us,
what is God like? This is the subject of the next chapter.

Chapter 2

God the Creator

*Science describes how the world took
shape. The doctrine of creation
affirms that all things were made by
God, that he is in control of his creation,
and it is good.*

You have probably seen one of those old
editions of the Bible with dates printed in the margin:
Paul converted on the road to Damascus, A.D. 35, the
Jews taken into captivity in Babylon, 593 B.C., and
most obvious of all, on the first page of Genesis: the
creation of the world, 4004 B.C. You will not likely
find these dates in any Bible printed today, but they
stood in thousands of Bibles printed in the nineteenth
century, appearing to many readers as if they had the
authority of God behind them. Actually they had something a little less than divine authority: the sanction of
the Anglican Archbishop Ussher, who worked them out
in the middle of the seventeenth century. Quite how

his dates got into the Bible no one seems to know. How they got out is a matter of painful recollection to us all.

1. SCIENCE AND THE DOCTRINE OF CREATION

Well before 1850, the advance of the science of geology had begun to throw doubt on Ussher's dates. The existence of fossils of prehistoric animals embedded in the rocks, the stratification of these rocks themselves suggested that the world must be a great deal older than six thousand years. Of course people could close their minds to the facts and say like Sir Edmund Gosse's father that the world was created in the year 4004 with the fossils in it. That kind of ostrich behaviour wasn't good enough. When Charles Darwin published his book, the *Origin of Species*, in 1859, the game was up, and Ussher's dates had to go. Since then, I fear that the first chapter of Genesis, and the doctrine of creation, have been an embarrassment to many Christian people.

That is a great pity, because the doctrine of creation is a basic Christian belief.

The whole struggle between science and religion over the first chapter of Genesis was a mistake and need never have occurred. There were thinkers at the time who saw that, but they were not listened to. There had been theologians centuries before, who, if they had been heard, could have prevented a great deal of the harmful confusion, because they knew, and said in their published works, that the doctrine of creation is not a scientific theory. Here are two examples:

—As far back as 1497, Dean Colet, a great English churchman, who lived not only before Darwin and

Newton, but also before Copernicus, realized that the first chapter of Genesis did not pretend to be either science or history.

—Two centuries earlier, around 1270, the great mediaeval theologian, Thomas Aquinas, was teaching his students that there was no reason why a scientist, as a *scientist*, should not believe that the world was eternal, and that the doctrine of creation was a theological proposition, to be held by faith alone.

Now I do not mean, any more than did Thomas Aquinas, to indulge in theological double-talk. I do not mean that a thing can be true in science and false in religion. What I do mean is that the doctrine of creation is totally misunderstood if it is thought of as a scientific theory or as a play by play description of how the physical world came into being. It has often been misunderstood in that way—in all ages of the church. But I don't believe that ever was the true purpose of the doctrine.

The doctrine of creation is not a scientific description of how the physical universe took shape. It is a theological description of how God was, and is, and always will be related to the whole of nature. God is Creator; everything else is his creation. The whole of reality can be divided without remainder into these two classes: Creator and creation.

When it is looked at in this way, the idea of creation is neither opposed to science nor threatened by the advance of scientific knowledge.

The best way of showing what the doctrine is not is to try to show what it really is.

2. GOD CREATED OUT OF NOTHING

An old catechism asks: "What do you believe when you say: I believe in God, the Father Almighty, Maker of heaven and earth?"

The answer begins: "[I believe] that the eternal Father of our Lord Jesus Christ made, out of nothing, heaven and earth and all that in them is. . . ."

The doctrine of creation teaches that God made *out of nothing* heaven and earth and all that in them is: and the words "out of nothing" are very important. You will not find them in the first chapter of Genesis. Indeed it is doubtful if the phrase can be found in the scriptures at all, but it is basic to the doctrine, and from very early times the deliberate teaching of the church has always said that the very essence of creation as Christians understand it, is making out of nothing. Why has this been said and why has it been insisted on century after century?

If Mrs. Smith goes down town, buys herself a few yards of material and a printed pattern and runs up a dress on her sewing machine, you would say that she had *made* a dress. If Mrs. Brown goes down town and buys herself a fifteen dollar dress off the rack, you might ask her where it was *manufactured*, in Toronto or Montreal or New York. But if Mrs. Jones spends two hundred dollars on a gown that came from Christian Dior's salon in Paris, it would be more than your life is worth to ask where it was manufactured or who made it. You would have to say, "Oh, my dear, what a stunning *creation!*"

Why do we say this about reputed works of art? Why do we talk about artistic creations? Because we feel that something really new has come into being. If a painter paints the front room you can calculate the cost at so much for paint and so much for labour, but you would be insulting an artist who had painted your portrait if you paid him so much for paints, so much for the canvas, and so much for his time. The artist is supposed to be in a small way a creator; he creates something that was not there before, something that could not happen naturally or by accident, something quite new.

Now, strictly and theologically speaking, not even the greatest artist is really a creator. He has to use something to express himself—paint or pencil, human words or musical notes. Even the most creative artist is also from one point of view a humble craftsman, a mere maker of things. But this is not so of God. He is a pure creator. His work is a pure creative act. He alone really creates out of nothing. He alone achieves pure and perfect expression of his purpose.

3. THERE IS NO OTHER EQUAL TO GOD

Someone may object, "I still don't see why it should be necessary to say that God creates out of nothing. Why couldn't God just have made the world like a great craftsman?"

Think: if anyone says that God made the world out of dust or out of water or out of fire or out of electricity, the next question is bound to be, "And where did they come from?" There is no indignity about an artist, even the world's greatest artist using brushes and paints and canvas made by someone else. But you simply can't say that about God. Not at least about the God of the

Bible. You see, if God did not create the world out of nothing, but made it or manufactured it out of something, that something must either have been made by someone other than God or must be itself eternal.

Neither of these alternatives can for a moment be accepted. For if there is somebody else, independent of God, who made it, then God is not all in all, but there is somebody outside of him, co-eternal with him, co-equal with him, another god in fact. Such an idea is intolerable to Jews and to Christians who have made it the basis of their creed that "the Lord our God is one." We would be back in polytheism, the worship of many gods, back to the darkness of paganism which trembles in fear because it does not know whether the world is actually under control, or whether two or more gods are fighting over it.

It would be no better to say that the material out of which God made the world had just always been there, for that would make matter itself co-eternal with God. Matter would be another god, and there we would be again with two gods on our hands, not knowing which one to believe in.

To put all of that into theological shorthand, *the doctrine of creation out of nothing is a repudiation of dualism.* But what's wrong with dualism? Christians (and Jews) believe that only one thing is ultimately real and eternal and true and good, namely God, and that all other things come from God. Dualism (two-ism) teaches that there are *two things* which are both ultimately real and eternal, whether you call them spirit and matter, light and darkness, or the good god and the bad god.

There are some very attractive things about dualism. It provides a simple explanation of evil in human life, and in nature, too, for that matter. If you are worried about why there should be pain and suffering and wickedness in a world which is supposed to have been created by a good God and to be ruled by him, you have plenty to worry about, and it is not easy to find an answer. But if you are a dualist you have a neat explanation right to hand: there is evil in the world because of the struggle between good and evil or light and darkness. God did the best he could with what he had to work on.

The only trouble about being a dualist is that there is no reason to suppose that good will ever win out. Indeed if darkness and evil are just as real as light and good, and just as eternal, the only thing one can look for is an endless, unresolved, meaningless struggle. Then there is no reason why anybody should be on one side rather than the other. Dualism explains evil, but only at the cost of making life meaningless. No Christian can be a dualist, and that is one reason why the church has always taught that God created the world out of nothing, that it is totally his creation, and that it is good.

In the first chapter of Genesis, after each act of creation, God looked at what he created and saw that it was good. At each stage this was repeated. And at the end God looked at the whole thing and behold, it was not only good, but very good, and God was pleased with what he had created. That is an important point. It is a supreme act of faith to say that, a declaration of faith in the dignity of nature and the

goodness of God. Without this, our whole Western
attitude towards nature, including our Western science,
could not have begun.

So the doctrine of creation out of nothing is not just
a piece of bad science, nor even a piece of antiquated
science, but a piece of good important theology, indeed
a doctrine on which all our lives are based, whether we
know it or not. I have tried to prove that by showing
that it is a denial of dualism. It is also a denial of
monism (or one-ism).

4. THE UNIVERSE IS NOT ITSELF GOD

I said that if God did not create the world out of
nothing then there must be something else, co-equal
with God and co-eternal with him. But there is another
possibility, another alternative to creation out of
nothing, and that is that the world itself is divine. That
may seem strange to you, but it is the basis of many
philosophies and religions, for example, Hinduism. A
pious Hindu would be prepared to say that if we only
had eyes to see and minds to understand, we ourselves
and all nature are really God; that God is just a name
for the sum total of all that is.

I tried to show the difference between dualism and
the biblical belief in God the creator by referring to
the problem of evil. And I tried to show that dualism
can easily explain why there is evil, but makes evil
ultimate and unredeemable and therefore hopeless.
Now I think we can see the difference between monism
and belief in God the Creator by again referring to the
problem of evil. When the monist faces the evils of the
world he tries to persuade himself that they are not

real at all, that all things are good, that all things are God, that evil is really an illusion, and the thing to do with illusions is not to fight them but to raise yourself above them and convince yourself that they are not real.

When you come to think of it, the hundreds of thousands of people in our society who have given themselves to the struggle against evil must have some very curious beliefs. On the one hand, they must believe that evil is terribly wrong, an offense against the nature of reality, something that must always be fought against. On the other hand they must believe that, although that fight has been going on all through our history without evil being finally overcome, in the end it will be overcome and the fight be victorious. In other words, they reject both the monist view that evil is illusion and the dualist view that evil is eternal.

Why do they do so? Not because of anything science tells them, for science has little or nothing to say about good and evil. Nor is it because of anything history tells them, for history does not prove in any conclusive way that the world is getting better or that evil is being overcome. The people who fight against evil do so in fact because they believe this world is good and it is good because God created it.

In other words, they believe that evil is real and not an illusion. They believe God is against evil and able to overcome it in his own good time. And they believe that to be on God's side is to be on the side of good and against evil.

Multitudes of worthy people don't really know what they believe, but their hearts are on the side of goodness. If they understood the Christian doctrine of creation, they would stand up and say with a clear and steady voice, "I believe in God, the Father Almighty, Maker of heaven and earth." And how much happier and more effective they would be if they could say that, for then they could see why it is they do the things they do.

5. WHAT THE DOCTRINE OF CREATION MEANS FOR US

So far, I have been trying to show that the doctrine of creation out of nothing is not a piece of bad science, and that it is a serious statement of the sovereignty of God which guards against the hopelessness of dualism and the illusions of monism. I have tried to show, too, that like every real issue in theology it is something that profoundly affects the way we live. Now let us think of some practical ways in which all this makes a difference.

The doctrine of creation *helps us to pray.* If dualism were the truth, we could pray to God, but only in the way in which a pagan prays to an idol, hoping that we would get what we wanted out of God, always watching out of the corner of our eye for the other god who may interfere with what is going on, and ready to switch sides and start praying to the other if we thought that would work better. If dualism were the truth, God could not be trusted and relied on. Even if he were a good, kind, well-disposed god, he would not be the only god and not in full control of the universe. He would not be a god in whom one could put one's trust or to whom one could commit oneself without any holding back.

On the other hand, if monism were the truth, you could not pray to God at all. You could only pray to yourself. There are people who pray only to themselves or to the divine in their own souls. They do not and cannot pray to God for help or for grace or for guidance. All they can do is to blow on the sacred flame in their own hearts till it bursts out. They are the people who have to save themselves. For them there is no grace, only works.

The doctrine of creation *helps us to have a sound attitude towards body and spirit*. Spirit is supposed to be the good principle and body the bad, and life is thought of by dualists as an endless warfare between body and spirit. There are those who think that this is the Christian idea, but it certainly is not. It is thoroughly pagan. After Plotinos died it was said of him, "He was as though ashamed of being in a body." That was supposed to be the mark of a high, spiritual nature in his non-Christian circles.

Christians have a different viewpoint. If God is our Creator then he made our bodies as well as our souls and there is nothing godless about our bodily instincts, such as sex. It has often been thought that the body is the source of sin, but against this view the doctrine of creation stands fast. Sin is not the prerogative of the body. On the contrary, the Bible tends to speak of sin as being a spiritual more than a bodily thing. "The heart is deceitful above all things, and desperately wicked" (Jer. 17: 9). Sin is a spiritual problem and it can't be solved by abolishing the body.

All through the centuries there have been ascetic movements directed at the discipline or restraint of the body. Christian hermits in the desert in the third century starved themselves and nearly drove themselves crazy trying to subdue the body. One of them is supposed to have sat for thirty years on top of a pillar trying to become a saint. We feel there is something wrong about this, but there has also been something right and healthy about much monasticism and Puritanism. How are we to judge? The doctrine of creation helps us. If God created us body and soul, then anything that denies the body its rights is setting itself against God's work. God gave us bodies and we ought to accept them reverently and use them reverently. Minds are no more spiritual than bodies. Intellectual work is no more spiritual or more pleasing to God than working with your hands. It is an error to think so. True Christian asceticism isn't a denial of the body but a discipline of it. The monks said that to work is to pray, and the Puritans stressed the dignity of labour. We take these things for granted now, but they all go back to sound doctrine, and without sound doctrine we will not keep them.

The doctrine of creation *helps us to have a sound view of ourselves.* Pascal said the trouble with people who do not believe in God is that they tend to swing back and forth between despair and wild self-confidence. When everything goes well they are filled with confidence in men's divine powers and feel that they can be gods to themselves. When things go badly they feel that the world has fallen into chaos and has become the battlefield on which the gods fight out their own wars, trampling mankind under foot.

But if we believe in God, the Father Almighty, Maker of heaven and earth, we know that we are creatures; and if creatures, we are neither gods ourselves nor are we god-forsaken. As creatures of the one true God, we can be both humble and dignified, humble because we are always dependent on him, dignified because we are the work of his hands and the people of his care.

Believing in God as Creator we can think of ourselves as creatures. This is to say, we can accept the fact that we are not God without being resentful. We can accept the fact that there are limits to our powers, that there are many things we cannot do as well as other people or even can't do at all. But knowing all this, we can still rejoice in what God has given us, play the game to the end, use our talents to the full, and commit all we do to a wise Creator.

The biblical faith in God as Creator is nobly expressed in the prayer of Ezra:

> Thou art the Lord, thou alone; thou hast made heaven, the heaven of heavens, with all their host, the earth and all that is on it, the seas and all that is in them; and thou preservest all of them; and the host of heaven worships thee (Neh. 9: 6).

This is a great faith to declare, a faith not only in God, but in God's universe, and in the good purpose that runs through creation. It is not an unreasonable faith. It is not an anti-scientific belief. But it is a faith, believing where we cannot fully prove. Those who hold it are convinced that it makes more sense than any other view, more sense of the facts of the universe, and more sense of our life.

Chapter 3

The Living God

*The infinite God can be personal too.
If he is not, he is somehow less
than man. By a venture of faith we
discover the living God to whom
the Bible bears witness.*

While it is a long step forward in faith to be able to believe in God as the Creator of the world, this alone would not be enough to sustain a vital religion. One might be filled with awe and reverence before the infinite power of the Creator, and still feel that he must be so great and so far off that he can have no concern for the life of man. So the faith of the Bible goes on to affirm that he is a living God.

1. NOT THE GOD OF THE PHILOSOPHERS

When that brilliant scientist Pascal died, his friends found sewn into the lining of his coat a piece of paper on which he had written of his conversion experience.

Among other things it said this: "The God of Abraham, Isaac, and Jacob; not the God of the philosophers. . . ."

What did Pascal mean by this? He meant that the God of the Bible, God as he had come to know him, is a living, personal God, and not an abstract and impersonal idea.

Abraham and all the prophets were in revolt against idolatry. So were the philosophers of ancient Greece and India. So are most philosophers today. They refused to call the sun and the moon divine or to worship the powers of nature as gods. They would not allow anything on earth to be called divine, only God himself.

Whereas the people of the Bible continue to speak of God in personal terms, the great philosophers have tended to have a strictly impersonal view of God. They use a variety of impersonal words for God: the Absolute, Being, Nature, the One, the Good, and so on. They often think it a mark of childishness on the part of Christians to persist in speaking of God in personal terms.

Certainly there are difficulties in believing that God is personal. But despite all difficulties and temptations to change, the Jewish and Christian traditions have never yielded at this point. They have insisted that God is to be spoken of as HE, not as IT. He should be addressed as Thou, and not just discussed as the Absolute. However childish it may sound to the learned, one must think of God as speaking and acting. The essential difference between the God of the philosophers and the God of Abraham is this: the God of the philosophers is an idea they talk about; the God of the Bible is a person you talk with.

2. OBJECTION: MAN MAKES GOD IN HIS OWN IMAGE

One of the commonest objections made to the idea that God is personal is that we are just inventing a picture of God to suit ourselves and in the picture we make he looks very much like ourselves. They say that our God is a glorified father-image. How do we know he is like a person, they ask? Why should the cows not think of God as a cow or the fishes imagine a fish heaven? And aren't they just as likely to be right as we? This criticism was well put by Don Marquis:

> As the forehead of Man grows broader,
>   So do his creeds;
> And his gods they are shaped in his image,
>   And mirror his needs. . . .

There is a certain amount of justification for this criticism. Religion *has* emerged from some very crude and childish beginnings. The 'creeds', or religious convictions of man *have* grown broader with time. This of course proves nothing about the truth or falsity of religion. Everything man knows has developed in the same way, including his science and medicine, his mathematics and engineering. As more truth becomes known we revise our thinking, but we do not throw overboard the wisdom of the past.

There seems to be some justification also for the criticism that man's gods are shaped in his image. The gods of the heathen religions were all too human. And the idea of God that many of us held in our childhood was no doubt all too human. Many adults in the Christian church probably picture him as being something like a good-natured old grandfather endowed with supernatural powers, and we need to outgrow some of the childish limitations of such a picture of God.

This does not mean, however, that we ought to give up the idea of God as personal and living. There is a truth here that must be preserved, without which our picture of God *would* be too small.

When we speak of God as speaking and acting, we do not mean that he speaks and acts in the same way that men do. He is not a Father or a King or Judge in the way that men are. To speak of him as the Absolute, implying that he has no real concern with the life which he has created on the earth would be far more misleading.

Is this important? It is when you think of prayer and forgiveness. If God is impersonal, prayer can never be anything more than private meditation, a conversation with ourselves. If God is impersonal, forgiveness can never be anything more than accepting ourselves and learning how to live with other people.

If personal relations are at the heart of things, and love and forgiveness, devotion and sacrifice among the most real and important things there are, then it is natural to believe that these personal human experiences give us a real clue to the nature of God. If the best things we see in personality are lacking in God, then man is in some ways greater than God. This is absurd.

So we feel it is reasonable to believe that God can not be *less* than personal, though he may well be more. And if it appears to some that man makes God in his own image, the answer is that while we believe God is much greater than we can know or understand, we have to picture him in terms of the highest we know, and to picture him as less than personal is not good enough.

3. OBJECTION: IT IS CONTRADICTORY TO SAY GOD IS BOTH INFINITE AND PERSONAL

Science has so vastly expanded our view of the universe that if we think of God at all it must be in terms of infinity. The vastness of space, the immense span of time, the numberless host of stars, make us realize that the God who created and creates all this must be wise and powerful and great beyond all our imagining. So the objection is raised that we are expecting something quite unreasonable when we dare to hope that this infinite God cares for man and responds to his cry. It is said that it is a contradiction, a paradox, to speak of God as infinite and at the same time personal.

There is in fact no contradiction. Only a God who is infinitely great could be able to concern himself at one and the same time with stars and atoms, with the universe and you.

A casual visitor to the home of Dr. Claris E. Silcox, might well be bewildered at the extent of his library, which filled three rooms of his big old Toronto house. But those who knew him well realized that he knew and valued each one of them, and knew just where to find the ideas he wanted for his wide-ranging lectures and articles on social and religious life in Canada. The breadth of his mind and the extent of his memory made every book a part of his concern. Likewise it is because of the greatness of God that he can be personally concerned with us.

4. VENTURE AND RESPONSE

Even if we can satisfy our minds or the minds of others with solid arguments to show that belief in the

living God is reasonable, something more is needed.
Belief in God is something more than reason. It
requires a commitment. It is called by some a gamble,
or the leap of faith into the darkness of the unknown.
I would rather call it a venture. For though it involves
a certain risk, and means going beyond what can be
proved, it is not a blind risk. It is made in response to
certain feelings. These are clues to truth.

Suppose a stranger comes to you and asks you to do
something which demands an immediate decision. You
are staying alone in a farmhouse on a winter's night.
The stranger knocks at your door and asks you to come
out to the highway and help an injured man. Is he
telling the truth? Or is he a crook? You have to make
up your mind whether to trust him or not. It is risk,
but not blind risk, for you have some indications. You
can judge by what the man looks like, how he talks,
by the impression he makes on you. Either way you
have to make a venture, one of faith or one of unbelief,
and a great deal may be at stake.

In a sense you are testing the stranger. In another
sense he is testing you. And the response that you make
to him, like faith in God, is a personal commitment.

Jesus told a story about a man who had two sons
(Matt. 21: 28-31). He went to the first and said, "Son,
go and work in the vineyard today." And the son
answered, "I will not." But afterwards he repented and
went. Then the father went to the second son and said
the same. He answered, "I'm going, sir." But he did
not go. "Which of the two," asked Jesus, "did the will
of his father?"

So venture and response go together. And sometimes it is only after we have ventured to commit ourselves to trust in God that we find that we have done so in response to the stirring of his Spirit within us.

5. THE WITNESS OF SCRIPTURE

Those of us who have been raised in Jewish or Christian traditions seldom realize how extraordinary the Bible is. When you set it beside the sacred writings of any other religion the difference is astonishing. Most other sacred writings are full of myths and legends, or philosophic speculations, or tedious moralizings. But the Bible is the record of the experiences of a people in touch with the living God over a period of two thousand years.

That is an immense body of experience, sifted and tested and thought through, and handed down to us because it is of lasting and priceless value. The Bible piles story upon story, incident upon incident, to demonstrate that God is a living God, one who has a purpose for human life, one who is concerned for the righteousness and welfare of his people. The Bible bears witness to the God who speaks. And it bears witness to the difference it makes in the lives of men when they respond to the living God, whether they accept him or reject him.

So it is for good reasons, and as a venture of faith, and supported by the experience of age after age, that we believe in a personal God.

Can we also say he is a loving God? To that question we turn next.

Chapter 4

The Love of God

Love's many meanings cannot all express
what the love of God is like. His love
is not the passion to possess but
the lovingkindness that bestows
When this divine love touches us we
begin to love in like fashion.

"God is Love, I dare say. But what a mischievous devil Love is." So said Samuel Butler, one of those good, old-fashioned, drum-beating Victorian atheists who did so much to enliven the religious life of his time. At first sight the statement looks rather blasphemous. The only thing that stops one calling it blasphemy is that unfortunately it appears to be true. We cannot read the newspaper for two days together without being forced to admit that love is a mischievous devil and causes a vast amount of damage in human relations.

39

1. THE MANY MEANINGS OF LOVE

Just think what happens. The body of a girl is found in a ditch. The police arrest a young man and charge him with murder. "Why did you do it?" they ask. He answers, "It was love."

An elderly couple celebrating their golden wedding tell the newspaper reporter how happy they are. "To what do you attribute your happy married life?" "I guess you'd call it love."

A great musician has just given a triumphal recital. He is asked about himself. How many hours a day does he practise? Eight or ten. How long has this gone on? Since he was a child. When will he be able to stop practising? Never. Why does he do it, for fame or money? Oh yes, that is pleasant, but ambition alone would not have kept him going. What keeps him going? The love of his art.

Or think of this: a young mother has an abnormal child. It does not grow and develop as children should. The mother cares for her child with endless patience and tenderness. Her friends and neighbours marvel that all her sacrifice does not make her embittered. They do not ask why. They know that this also is love.

I wonder if there is any word in our language so badly overworked as the word love, or any word which has such an amazing range of meanings. It is a real defect in a language not to have different words to describe the mercy and the lovingkindness of God on the one hand and on the other the sexual passion that may drive men to ecstasies or despair.

The Greeks had a word for most things and they needed three words where we have only one. In order to avoid confusion, it helps us to borrow the Greek words; and so we have:

Agape — compassionate love (pronounced ah-ga-pay),
Eros — the love of desire and aspiration,
Philia — the love of friendship.

2. THE LOVE OF FRIENDSHIP

Philia is the love between equals, the love of friendship, comradeship and companionship. It may be united with other kinds of love, in happy marriages, for instance. But it may be seen at the clearest between friends, who rely on one another, treat one another as equals. It may not be very exalted or very exciting, but it is a comfortable kind of love. In its way *philia* is a type of love that makes the world go round. So much of our daily life depends on it. It provides so much of the cement of society. It has sometimes been called economic love because of its mundane, business-like quality. But it is good and we need it.

Only it is not religious. At least when we talk about the love of God it cannot be *philia* that we mean. *Philia* is love between equals and God has no equals. He needs no one to support him: no friend to comfort him. People sometimes do think of God that way; they try to bribe God or make bargains with him: "Look, O God," they say, "I am offering you this wonderful sacrifice, now help me to be successful." But this is a degradation of religion, not true religion.

3. THE LOVE OF DESIRE

The love of desire is indicated by *eros*. This is a strong urge, a desire, a compulsion. It may lead to romance, but it may lead to the criminal court, when for one reason or other it becomes the mischievous devil that Butler spoke of.

The basis of this kind of love is need, physical and psychological need, which drives one literally into the arms of someone else who can supply that need. It is not wrong that it should be so. God gave us these needs and urges and properly channelled they provide the natural basis for the family.

The pagan religions pictured their gods as having this kind of love. In the legends of Greece and Scandinavia the gods seem all too human in this respect. One of the reasons the old religions died out was that men came to see that this kind of love did not properly belong to supernatural beings. The God who made the world can have no such needs and urges as we think of in connection with *eros* love, the love of desire that seeks to possess its object.

4. THE LOVE OF ASPIRATION

There is another meaning of *eros* love that has definite religious importance. That is the kind of love that desires some ideal object. This is the upreach of the mind for truth, of the soul for beauty, goodness or for God. This is aspiring love. Whole religions have been built on this idea of love.

Aristotle the great Greek philosopher had this idea. We don't have to be philosophers to get his point. He believed literally that it was this kind of love that makes the world go round, even that it was the love of God that makes the world go round. How does God make the world go round? Aristotle answers: not by loving the world, but by being loved.

We all know how a pretty girl can make the boys run after her. Just by being what she is she moves them. She may not even know the stir she is creating or how many hearts she has moved. Well, said Aristotle, on a much higher level, on a spiritual level, God is like that. Just as the beloved object moves the lover by the desire it awakes, so God moves the world *by being loved*. God does not have to do anything. He does not have to love the world. He just has to be what he is and he draws all the world after him. He does not even have to know that the world exists.

There is something very impressive about this idea of God in his majestic and solitary blessedness drawing the world after him in rapture and adoration, moving others and yet unmoved, like a magnet drawing us all into its field. In Aristotle's view we love God and the whole world loves God because he is perfect. We could not love him as we do unless he were perfect. And if God were to love us in return it would spoil everything, for it would show that he was not really perfect after all.

If *eros* is the basis of true love, then love must always be for what is higher than ourselves: it is desiring, aspiring love and we cannot desire or reach up towards anything that is not better than we are.

We could put the point in a fairy tale: A poor servant girl loves a handsome prince. Each day as he rides past on his horse she looks out the cellar window and is lost in admiration. One day by chance she meets him in the

street and curtseys to him, and he, noticing her there
with her poor, thin, dirty, ugly face, takes her by the
hand and leads her home to the palace. As she goes,
her mind is in turmoil. What does it mean? He cannot
long for her as she longs for him; he would have to be
mad or under a spell to long for such a poor, ugly
creature. If he were mad he could no longer be her
ideal; it would spoil everything. No, he can't love me
as I love him, I could not want him to. Perhaps he
just wants me to clean his boots, or scrub the pans in
the kitchen.

5. The love of compassion

So, if *eros* love is all the love there is in the spiritual
world, those who love God cannot wish that God should
love them in return. If *eros* love is all the love there
is in the spiritual world, a text like "God so loved the
world that he gave his only begotten Son" would be
impossible and meaningless. Why should God love the
world? What beauty is there about us that he should
desire us? No beauty at all. If it were even to be said
that God loves us it would have to be by a new kind of
love.

If there had not been a new kind of love there could
never have been any Christianity, for God could not
have done what we believe he did do in Christ without
something more. And without something more Christianity could not have been understood or even
imagined. But there was something more—a new kind
of love—which made itself known in the world by
chance or by providence (depending on your point

of view) in time to make the expression of the gospel possible. It came in the Old Testament.

Jehovah in the Old Testament is a fierce, angry God, jealous, wrathful, crude, and primitive. Many who fancy themselves modern and enlightened enjoy looking down their noses at the Old Testament and contrasting it with the more spiritual views of God which they and the New Testament hold together. There is only one excuse for such a mistake and that is ignorance. The Old Testament does speak of God's wrath and his righteousness, but it also speaks very movingly of his love. Take just one verse: Isaiah 63: 9.

> In all their affliction he was afflicted . . . in his
> love and in his pity he redeemed them; . . . and
> carried them all the days of old.

Here was a new kind of love indeed and a new understanding of God. Not the remote and cold and majestic God of Aristotle who is the object of his people's love but unable to love them back, but a God who has compassion for his people, who follows them with his love and care, who pleads with them, reasons with them, forgives them, brings them back out of bondage and will never let them go. Here is what we all know now as Christian love: what we know in our hearts to be the deepest love of all. And where do we find it? First, in the Old Testament, and then supremely in the New.

When the Old Testament was first translated into Greek, the problem arose as to what word they were to use for this new kind of love. What they found was the word *agape*: an uncommon word which could be given a new meaning.

What that new meaning was we will see best if we contrast *agape* and *eros*. Perhaps the basic contrast between *eros* and *agape* is up and down.

eros —	is an upward movement
agape —	comes down
eros —	is the aspiration and longing for the high ideal, for perfection
agape —	is the reaching down in mercy and compassion for the poor, ugly, sinful and lost
eros —	is man's way up to God
agape —	is God's way down to man
eros —	seeks for itself the highest and the best
agape —	"seekest not its own"—it gives itself away
eros —	seeks to gain immortal, perfect, blessed life
agape —	dares to lose itself
eros —	is primarily man's love for God; God is the object of eros
agape —	is primarily God's love for men; God is agape
eros —	is not spontaneous, it is drawn out, evoked, motivated by the worth and the value of what is loved
agape —	loves the unlovely, it seeks out that which has no beauty and no goodness, it loves us while we are yet sinners. It does not love us because we are worth loving, it loves us in order that we may become worthy of the love that was given first
eros —	is work
agape —	is grace

It is this new kind of love, *agape,* which is central in the New Testament, in Jesus' teachings and Jesus' life.

> In this is love," said John, "not that we loved God but that he loved us" (1 John 4: 10).

Constantly Jesus speaks of this outgoing, sacrificial, unselfish love:

> He (God) makes his sun rise on the evil and on the good, and sends rain on the just and the unjust (Matt. 5: 45).

God does not wait for men to earn his love, nor does he dole out his love in rewards like a heavenly book-keeper. Just as the householder in the parable paid the labourers in his vineyard a whole day's salary even though many of them had not earned it, so God loves us though we are not worthy of his love (Matt. 20: 1-16).

Not only does Jesus speak of this love, he himself lived by it. As Paul said of him: "While we were yet helpless, at the right time Christ died for the ungodly. . . . God shows his *agape* for us in that while we were yet sinners Christ died for us" (Rom. 5: 6-8). "God so loved the world . . ." (John 3: 16).

This idea is so central to the New Testament and so familiar that it is only by a deliberate effort that we can see how different, how daring and how revolutionary it really is. People talk about Christian love as though it were a watered down version of real love, but quite the reverse is true and after all the hard work we have done we ought to be able to see it. Christian love, *agape,* is really God's love come down to earth. That is no figure of speech, it is literally true, and you can see it to be true.

What has happened in Christianity is that the ancient view of religion, as man's reaching up in love towards goodness, has entirely been turned around. You don't begin with human love, not even the highest human love, you begin with God who by some incredible miracle is said to love men first. God's love comes down, not only at Christmas but all the time. And all our response to God, and our compassion towards others, flows from this. Christian love is an imitation of God's love. Indeed it seems to happen because God's love has been poured into our hearts (Rom. 5: 5) it overflows into the lives of others. As Luther used to say, we are like a vessel or a tube through which the divine blessings must flow without intermission to other people.

So we believe that God is a God of love. And when we say this we do not mean a selfish or sentimental kind of love, but the kind of love that seeks to fulfil in man the good and divine purpose which the Creator first had in mind when he made man in his own image.

Chapter 5

God and Evil

*We cannot pretend that evil does not
exist. When evil does its worst, as in the
crucifixion of Jesus, God works out
his good purposes in spite of all.
With him we too can overcome
evil with good.*

A young man from a poor home was nearing the end of his college course. This was the day he and his parents had worked so hard and sacrificed so much to reach. Then suddenly he took ill and died.

One of his professors was telling this story to a friend, and the friend said, "Now, was it God who did that? Or was it the devil?"

He might have asked, "Or was it that the world is simply indifferent towards life and all the things we hold to be good?"

1. THE PROBLEM OF EVIL

Suffering and evil are facts of life that we cannot avoid. Even if they do not seem to strike us personally, for years at a stretch, they are present on every side. If we have any feeling at all for other people, their troubles concern us too. And whether the troubles are theirs or ours, the problem of evil forces itself upon us sooner or later with its perplexing questions.

The whole of religion, it has been said, is an attempt to answer these questions. Perhaps it would be more accurate to say that every religion tries in its own way to grapple with them and bring to man some way of dealing with the hard facts and the tragic events of life. Different systems of religion have very different ways of meeting the problem, and they cannot all be right.

Hinduism and Buddhism are both rooted in the conviction that to live is to suffer, and the chief end of man is to regard life as something to escape from. Only by losing oneself in the All, after a life of apathy, does suffering cease. At its base this is saying no to life.

The stream of religion that springs from the Bible accepts the reality of evil and suffering, but says the reality of God and his good purpose is greater than the reality of evil. It affirms that we are called to make the most of the good in life and combat evil in every way we can. At its base it is saying yes to life.

Because of this fundamental difference it is clear that if one of these systems is true in its interpretation of the fact of evil, the other cannot be true. This is not the place to explore the arguments for and against the negative view of life that underlies Hinduism. But the fact that such radically different views exist and claim the faith of millions is just one more reason why Christians ought to understand the insights of their own tradition.

It is a common experience among us that when adversity strikes we are not spiritually prepared to cope with it. So often we do not know what is the Christian attitude. We all know people who after some personal tragedy have come to a deeper and more mature religious faith, and can be said to have triumphed over the evil that befell them. We know also of people who, smitten by the blows of war or sickness, failure or bereavement, have been left bitter and hopeless.

What kind of a faith do we need to make us able to meet evil without becoming defeated?

2. THE CHRISTIAN ATTITUDE IS NOT EASY

I believe that Christianity in the long run answers the problem of evil as nothing else can. But in the short run it makes it more difficult.

When we claim that there is a good God, a wise Creator, who made all things well and who loves his people, we are pointing to the conviction which overcomes evil. We are at the same time making it harder to explain why there should be evil at all.

Let us acknowledge this frankly at the outset, and make it quite clear to ourselves what are some of the explanations that Christians cannot use.

(*a*) We cannot use, first of all, what is probably the oldest and shrewdest of all the solutions to the problem of evil: *the simple denial that evil is really evil at all.*

In every age of civilization there are people who insist that things which seem evil are not really so, but only good in disguise. Often these are very noble and dignified people. They are often said to be stoical, because of a group of people in the ancient world called Stoics who took this point of view.

One of the greatest Stoics, Seneca, used to say that no evil could ever befall a good man. "I will prove to you," he said at the beginning of one of his books, "that you ought never to feel sorry for a good man, for though people may call him miserable, he cannot be so." The good man is he who has raised himself above the things of the world, who has banished from himself all the sins that trouble weaker men. So strong in mind and soul is he that envy or jealousy or greed or any other kind of temptation simply cannot touch him. Such a man, says Seneca, is raised above evil. He may suffer, as others do, the loss of friends or family or reputation or goods. Disease and pain may rack him. But these things can no longer touch him: *they are not evil at all to him.*

Stoicism is overcoming evil by shutting one's mind against it. This may satisfy me, but only if I also shut my mind to the evil that others suffer. And that is selfishness.

How far this is from the way of Jesus! Morally perfect as he was, he never closed his mind to the cry of human need. He bore the sorrows and the sins of others on his heart. And he was not content until he had done all he could to relieve their need and overcome the evils that afflicted them.

If we believe that Jesus reveals the mind of God to us, and that his example and his command to love our neighbour are true guides for life, then we cannot accept the stoic answer to the problem of evil.

Christian Science and kindred sects have another
way of presenting the same kind of approach to evil.
They say that only mind is real, and mind can be
disciplined to think only true and good thoughts. This
being so it follows that pain, sickness, and even death
are unreal to the mind that is on the right track. There
appears to be much in this view that is wholesome and
optimistic. But the basic idea is false. Death is a fact.
Pain is a fact. And no amount of wishful thinking is
going to wipe them out of existence.

(*b*) There is a second simple answer to the problem
of evil that we as Christians have to give up: it is *that
God could prevent it if he would, but he won't.* Many
people who have looked at the tragedies and dis-
appointments of life have come to the sad conclusion
that God or the gods or whatever powers rule our lives
have no mercy and no concern for us, that they play
with us as boys play with butterflies, pulling them to
pieces, half in cruelty, half in ignorance.

We may in moments of extremity be tempted to
think that way, as Job was when he cried out in his
agonies that God must be a wild beast who is gnashing
his teeth at us (Job 16: 9), or as Jeremiah was when
he accused God of being a deliberate deceiver. But we
know, even as we say these things, that they are a
temptation and must be put aside.

There is another, less obnoxious, way of solving the
problem of evil by blaming it on God. We could say,
as people have often said, that God made the world
and set it on its way but now leaves it to look after
itself. If there is evil in life that is all part of the game
and we must fight it alone. There may be a good deal

of truth in this. God does seem to allow some evil to come to us, and no doubt we are supposed to fight it. But that we fight alone we cannot believe. The Christian gospel clearly teaches that evil is a good deal more serious than that, more tragic than that, so serious and tragic indeed that it involves God himself, who comes in Christ to fight for us and with us and who himself suffers as grievously as we. If God himself bears with us in our struggle with evil, if he himself is involved in it, then we certainly cannot explain evil by saying that God does not bother to do anything about it.

(c) This brings us to a third simple answer to the problem of evil which we as Christians have to forego. We cannot explain the evils and tragedies of life by saying *that God would prevent them if he could, but can't.*

Many people have said this too from age to age, but it really means giving up faith in God altogether. If you read the classical plays of Greece, plays like *Oedipus Rex,* you can see one of the great spiritual problems of that age. It was this: "Do the gods really rule over our lives? Or are we all controlled by some dark inhuman power called fate?" The tragedy of ancient Greece was that in the end fate won out. People came to believe that even the gods could not control fate. Once this was accepted the gods simply faded away. They became part of the conventional furniture of life. People put up statues to them, and referred to them in public speeches, but the gods were dead. They were useless. They had been proved to be a fraud.

People often say that this is happening to us, that
we really believe in fate too, that our God is dead or
dying, and when we face the possibility of a third
world war we just feel hopeless. We don't believe that
any one person or nation will start it, but that some
blind, merciless, meaningless force is bringing it on us
and nothing can be done about it. There is no use
trying to stop it, there is no use praying about it, it
will just come.

Some people seem to have come to believe this. They
have lost faith in men and in God. They believe things
are beyond our control, they are meaningless, and we
must therefore despair. A good many people came to
this sad state at the end of the last war. Everything
they believed in had collapsed, or had shown itself
unable to save, and if you want to know what it feels
like to come to this, read George Orwell's *1984* or a
book called *The Twenty-Fifth Hour*. Needless to say,
anyone who has got this far has ceased to be a Christian. Anyone who can accept this kind of despair has
decided that God is an idol, and Christianity an
illusion.

Anyone who has come to a despairing conclusion of
this sort has of course a very complete and adequate
explanation of evil. Why should there not be evil and
meaninglessness, tragedy and frustration if the world
is just a chance bunch of atoms careering about space
without observing the speed limits? Why should there
not be evil if history is only a chapter of accidents?
Why should there not be evil if God is only a kind-
hearted old soul sitting up in heaven filled with good-

will, but not knowing what to do next? If all that were true, there would be nothing left for us but to make ourselves comfortable for the duration of our lives, or of the world, whichever be the shorter.

I expect we all have our moments of despair about the world. Next time you have one of these spells just ask yourself whether you seriously believe that the whole of life is a meaningless accident, that things are not ruled by God but by chance. If you decide that life is meaningless, well, don't commit suicide without consulting a minister first. But if you simply can't believe that, as I can't, then draw the conclusion that your despair (and the moments of despair that we all know) is a temptation to lose faith in God, to abandon him and your fellow man. We all suffer temptations. Even Christ did. And we all give way to them, though he did not. But there is forgiveness with God for this and for all our sins.

So let us not take our despair too seriously, and let us not think that all hope has gone. The moment when we are tempted to despair is often the moment when we discover to our surprise that we do believe in God after all.

3. MEETING EVIL IN PRACTICE

By this time you are perhaps beginning to think we have worked ourselves into such a tight corner that we will never get out. Yet every day, where you live, there are Christian people who are proving by the way they face the trials of life that the problem has been solved. Have you ever gone to visit some sick person afraid that you would find him depressed, upset, and hopeless, not knowing what you would do or say? And have you ever discovered that instead of cheering the patient up you were cheered up yourself? Such experiences help to convince me that Christianity is not a man-made religion but a gospel from God.

There are two ways of "solving the problem" of evil. One is to explain, if you can, why it is there. The other is to cope with it in life. People who trust in God are showing us every day how to cope with evil victoriously in practice.

Do you remember the story of Job in the Old Testament? He was a good, happy, prosperous man who suffered a terrible series of calamities. He lost everything. His friends came to him and said, "You must have done something pretty terrible or God would never have allowed this to happen to you." If Job had not been an unusually strong-minded man he would have accepted the explanation of his friends. He would have concluded that some terrible sin he had committed, perhaps unawares, had brought all this suffering upon him. He would just have settled down in dust and ashes and repentance to make the best of it all.

But Job *was* a strong-minded man. When he examined his conscience and found himself innocent of any great sin he simply refused to accept the suggestion of his friends that he was guilty. He refused to believe that suffering is a proof of sin or always comes as a punishment for sin. It may be that we bring a good deal of suffering on ourselves through our own folly or wickedness, but that doesn't explain it all.

As a matter of fact Job never really did "explain" the problem of evil. All he could say was, "Shall we receive good at the hand of God, and shall we not receive evil?" (Job 2: 10).

The book of Job is no reasoned argument to prove that God is just. It remains to the end an affirmation of faith. It gives no rational solution to the problem of evil. Indeed it is a systematic rejection of rational solutions. Job does not discover a *truth* about God or the world or the future. He encounters *God* and in so doing learns the truth about himself and his duty. He seeks an answer, but he finds God.

You may think that a rather commonplace answer, but just read the book of Job and see what it sometimes costs to reach a commonplace before it has become common.

Jesus had to fight this same battle all over again. In the story of the ninth chapter of John's Gospel, the disciples saw a man who had been born blind. They were just like Job's friends: they caught the scent of sin in their nostrils and they wanted to hunt it down. To have suffered such a terrible calamity a man must have done something really wicked. What could it have been? But, if he was born blind he couldn't be suffering for anything he himself had done in his own lifetime. Was he then suffering for some sin of his parents? Or something he had done in a previous existence? These were the questions they asked. Jesus would have nothing to do with such ideas. "It was not that this man sinned, or his parents, but that the works of God might be made manifest in him." And then he cured him.

How much there is in the Gospels about sickness and sick people! And how consistently Christ works against suffering and will never accept it! You know how easy it is to say of people in trouble, "Oh well, they probably deserve all they get." Perhaps they do, but that is not for us to judge. Our only duty is to fight evil where we find it and have compassion on men. That is the way our Lord himself acted. When you come to think of it, that is just the way our doctors and nurses act, too. They make no moral judgments. They simply regard it as their duty to serve God and men by fighting sickness. They don't stop to ask, "Why do these things happen?" They simply ask how can we cure them now that they have happened, and how can we prevent them happening again? I think that is exactly what our Lord wants them to do.

Still, you and I and the doctor want to know why these things happen, even if we seldom ask it out loud.

4. THE CRUCIFIXION

So we come to the heart of the whole matter. What brought things to a head and what makes Christians act as they do and believe as they do about the ways of God with men we find in the crucifixion of Jesus.

That was the worst thing that ever happened. Men had long been asking questions about the dreadful things that were allowed to happen in this world— things that made people wonder whether there was any meaning at all in human life, or any God in heaven. Now came the most dreadful thing of all, driving the sharp point of the problem deeper into the human heart than it had ever gone before—the crucifixion of Jesus.

Was it God that did that? Or was it the devil?

Of course it was the devil and all his hosts: the
jealousy of the Pharisees, the scheming of the Sadducees, the treachery of Judas, the hysteria of the
crowd; and behind all that the demonic powers of
darkness which "crucified the Lord of glory." The
men who wrote the New Testament are quite clear
about that. This was one thing that ought never to
have happened, the most godless thing that was ever
done in this wicked world, the crucifixion of Jesus.

But was that the whole truth? Is that all they had
to say about it? No indeed. All over the New Testament we find this extraordinary conviction that the
crucifixion of Jesus was not only the worst thing that
had ever been done, but also the best thing that had
ever happened. God was in it. Not in the sense that
God from his throne in heaven appointed this fate for
an innocent man called Jesus. But in the sense that
God was in Christ, and when he suffered and died on
the cross, this was God himself bearing the sin and suffering of the world. This was the victory of divine love,
this was the redemption of the world. In this evil was
overcome.

How can a thing be both bad and good? How could
the crucifixion be both an act of devilish wickedness
and a work of God's mercy? It is hard to understand.
Yet this is what Christians have always said. Think of
Peter preaching in Jerusalem within a few weeks of the
crucifixion and to the very people who saw it: "This
Jesus," he says, "you crucified and killed by the hands
of lawless men," yet he was "delivered up according
to the definite plan and fore-knowledge of God" (Acts
2: 23). You meant it for evil, but God meant it for good.

Paul was afflicted with some ailment which he referred to as a "thorn in the flesh." It must have been painful and troublesome, incurable by the medical science of the time, and it hindered Paul in his work. Now listen to the way he speaks of it:

> A thorn was given me in the flesh, a messenger of Satan, to harass me, to keep me from being too elated. Three times I besought the Lord about this, that it should leave me; but he said to me, "My grace is sufficient for you, for my power is made perfect in weakness." I will all the more gladly boast of my weaknesses, that the power of Christ may rest upon me.

We can see here how Paul with the instinct born of faith avoided all the wrong answers to the problem and turned them into right ones. First of all, he did not pretend that black was white. Like a healthy-minded man, he hated suffering and disease whether his own or other people's and he fought against it. He did not become a neurotic and nurse his wounds, nor did he imagine himself too high-minded to bother about them. He spoke of his own disease as "a messenger of Satan" and just as the Lord in his earthly life had struggled against the works of darkness, so did Paul.

Secondly, Paul did not allow it to embitter him or to destroy his faith and trust in God. He prayed about his infirmity. Three times, he says, he besought the Lord about it. And nothing happened. But if you had asked Paul whether his prayer went unanswered he would have said, "No, only I got an answer I didn't expect. God said to me that his grace was sufficient for me."

Baron von Hugel once wrote that Jesus cures pain and disease as though they could not be utilized, but he also teaches people to utilize pain and disease as though they could not be cured. That is what Paul and many others have discovered. While suffering is a bad thing in itself which nobody should want, yet it can make better men and women of us. It can bring a richness and a beauty to our lives which we cannot get in any other way.

The third thing is that Paul even came to the daring conclusion that it was God who had sent this trouble upon him. "There was given to me," he says, "a thorn in the flesh. . . ." Who gave it to him? God or the devil? Paul tells us in the same sentence, in the same breath, that somehow it was both. His troublesome malady was a messenger of Satan to buffet him, but it was also the gift of God to make a true man of him.

What a puzzle that is! How could anyone believe both of these things? Yet this is what Christian people manifestly do. They fight against disease and pain and death as though they were evils and yet they profit from them as though they were good. They fight evil and yet they know that it is only in a rough and tumble world of struggle against evil that human souls can be remade in the image of God.

No parent could wish that his son or daughter should suffer evils and temptations, and no parent could possibly take the responsibility of sending such things to his child. He knows nevertheless that only through suffering can character and eternal destiny be made. Although we begin by wondering how a good God can send evil on his people, we end by seeing that only a good God could be counted on to allow evil to exist. Only because we believe that God reigns, despite all the injustice and tragedy, can we profit from the injustice and tragedy even as we struggle against it.

The sorrows of life do not necessarily lead people to a nobler character. They lead some to bitterness and despair, others to hard selfishness. Only those who trust in God can come through unharmed. But the strange and wonderful thing about the Christian life is the way in which it seems to enable the saints to rebel against evil and to trust in God at one and the same time. They do not become bitter or defiant; and in the end they are hopeful and faithful people. Like the prophets of the Old Testament, they wrestle in their prayers with the God they love and their lives become one long active intercession.

What the Christian knows is how to believe in the goodness of God and rebel against the evils of life at one and the same time. We need faith, but a faith that rebels. Only if we are fighting evil can we praise God for his goodness without complacent self-satisfaction. Only if we affirm his goodness can we really believe the struggle against evil is worth while. It may seem like a contradiction, but we can say no less if we are to be true to our experience.

Chapter 6

Miracles

*If a miracle is a breach of natural law
it is a problem. But God works through
nature, and though an event may
have a natural explanation it can still
be miraculous if in it we see a
manifestation of the divine.*

An old lady from Southern Ireland was once crossing the border into Ulster. She said she had nothing to declare, but the customs men found in her baggage a green glass bottle, full, and well corked. She said it contained holy water, but the customs men, who were suspicious and hard-hearted Protestants, drew the cork. "Holy water, is it? Smells like whisky. What do you think?" The old lady sniffed cautiously; then her face lit up and she threw her hands in the air. "Glory be to God," she said, "it's a miracle."

There was a time when miracles were regarded as one of the great *proofs* of Christianity. Nowadays they are more likely to be a difficulty and even an embarrass-

ment, especially to young people. Those parts of the
Bible which are most suitable for use with children
are also the parts which contain the miracle stories.
Children may accept them when they are young, but
as they grow up under the influence of a scientific
education they begin to suspect them and either reject
Christianity as a collection of pre-scientific superstitions
or else carry into adult life an unresolved and painful
tension between their religious loyalty and their scientific conscience. Funny stories, like the one above, get
both their point and their pathos from this tension. I
am convinced that this tension is unnecessary, is the
result of defective theological teaching in the past, and
that the church has a duty to remove it.

1.   How MIRACLE BECAME A PROBLEM

The trouble has arisen not from any conflict between
science and the Bible, but *from the view of miracle
which defines it as a breach of natural law.* This false
(or at least misleading) view of miracle is in conflict
not only with science, but with the Bible itself. The
word "miracle" is not really a biblical word though it
is sometimes used in our English translations. The
Greek and Hebrew words which do occur in the biblical
text literally mean *sign, portent, wonder,* and *mighty
work.*

The idea that miracles are breaches of the laws of
nature is not a biblical idea and grew up much later.
How it did so is a long story which concerns the relations between theology and the changing scientific
theories of successive centuries.

For many centuries (one might say from the fourth
to the nineteenth) almost all Christians would have

explained miracles in this way. God, they would have said, is ultimately the cause of all things. He makes the sun to rise and the rain to fall as well as being the worker of miracles. The ordinary works of his providence take place in accordance with the laws of nature which he himself framed. Miracles, the extraordinary works of his providence, are caused by his direct intervention and not by the ordinary laws of nature.

This theory in one form or another satisfied generations of Christians including the scientists among them. Almost the only people who bothered to disagree with it were skeptics who claimed that nothing happened except by the laws of nature and that therefore miracles are to be dismissed as superstitious credulity.

There is one difference between Catholics and Protestants here. Catholics have traditionally claimed that miracles still happen, while many Protestants taught that the age of miracles is past, and only the miracles of the Bible are to be accepted. In saying this the Protestants were agreeing with the skeptics that contemporary accounts of miracles are to be dismissed as superstition. And it is not surprising that in time lively-minded Protestants began to ask why the biblical miracles should be given special treatment and defended against search for a natural explanation.

2. WHERE THE OLD VIEW WENT WRONG

This traditional theory has serious weaknesses both from the scientific and from the theological point of view.

By setting natural events in opposition to miracles, it tended to suggest that God was really active only in miraculous or supernatural events while natural events happened (so to speak) by themselves. This played straight into the hands of the atheists, because every time a scientific discovery was made and a natural explanation was furnished for some event that had not been understood, one more miracle story was exploded. The area in which God might be believed to be active was reduced. And God himself was gradually pushed out of the picture of the universe. As science advanced God seemed to be in retreat.

This was bad, not only from the religious point of view, but from the point of view of the scientists, most of whom were faithful Christians, and who were being put in the position of seeming to weaken religion whenever they were successful in the execution of their own proper task. What was almost as bad was that the theory encouraged some foolish theologians to oppose the proper work of science in the hope of protecting the miracles by preventing them from receiving a natural explanation.

All these evils resulted from a misuse of the traditional theory which was never intended to have such effects.

The traditional theory is not really faithful to the Bible itself. Many of the miracle stories of the Bible seem to have a natural explanation but are none the less regarded as signs and portents. The natural and the miraculous are not opposed or mutually exclusive. The crossing of the Red Sea by the Israelites was believed to be an act of God, and an extraordinary work of his providence, yet God is said to act through a natural cause—a strong east wind which blew the waters back

(Ex. 14: 21). The almond branch which Jeremiah saw (Jer. 1: 11) was quite normal and natural yet it was also a sign from God. For us a rainbow is a perfectly natural sight caused by the refraction of light. Yet to Noah it was a sign of God's mercy. The story of Elisha reviving the Shunammite's son by "lying upon the child, putting his mouth upon his mouth" (2 Kings 4: 34) may be an early case of artificial respiration by the mouth to mouth method. But if it were, that would not make it any less a sign of God's mercy and a wonder.

If this is true, then to make the absence of any natural explanation the essential thing about a miracle is to put the emphasis in the wrong place. What matters is that it is a work of God not that it is unnatural. *The attempt to distinguish between those works of God which happen naturally, and those which happen supernaturally is a mistaken one.* It does not really help us to interpret the Bible, nor does it fit the viewpoint of modern science.

There was a time when scientists were prepared to say that they knew more or less what things could happen naturally and what things could not. But in this age of sputniks, atomic reactors, and miracle drugs, one would have to be foolhardy to claim that certain things cannot happen naturally. If scientists nowadays speak about "the laws of nature" at all, it is only to give a generalized description of what has been observed, and they will usually insist that the descriptions will have to be revised from time to time.

This old theory has one curious result. If you insist on defining a miracle as something that has no natural cause then you will never be able to say for certain

that any given event is a miracle. At best you will only
be able to say that it looks like one, but of course the
scientists may explain it away tomorrow. This is a
ridiculous situation to be in. When Christians find
themselves hoping that the efforts of scientists to explain
and to describe nature will fail, and believing that God
will be glorified by that failure, something has gone
wrong somewhere. Such a situation would justify the
accusations of our enemies that Christianity is reactionary and opposed to truth.

What could be the reason for such a misunderstanding? One answer is the prevalence of the idea that in
miracles God acts independently of nature, with the
corresponding idea that in natural events, nature works
independently of God. This was never the teaching
of those who developed the traditional doctrine of
miracles, but it is what the doctrine came to mean
in the popular mind.

The idea that a miracle cannot have a natural
explanation seems to be at odds both with the Bible
and with modern science. We must look for a different
criterion.

3. A MIRACLE IS WHERE WE BEHOLD GOD

It is more useful to consider *a miracle as an event
in which God's being and power and nature are made
evident to the believer.* What makes a miracle is not
any supposed breach of the "laws of nature," but *the
manifestation of God.* Nature is God's creation. It is
always under his control and it is always demonstrating
his power to those who have eyes to see. The simplest
natural event the rain, the rainbow, the sky and the

clouds can do this, though they may not impress us because of their familiarity.

A miracle happens in that event or occasion in which we are jolted out of our complacency and see the hand of God in nature or history. We could always be seeing him, but our eyes are kept from recognizing him partly by our sin, no doubt, but also because God veils himself in his relations with men. It is only at special points in space and time that we "encounter" the God who is always present. A miracle makes us aware of something that is always true, that God is continually at work in nature and history.

A miracle is therefore of necessity unusual, startling, marvellous, wonderful. The New Testament speaks of wonders. But what makes them wonderful is *not* that they are breaches of natural law, but that they startle us into an awareness of God's presence and power. This is perhaps why Jesus so often refused to perform mere wonders to satisfy the idly curious. A miracle-event must be seen with the eyes of faith and must be seen as a sign, pointing to God at work in the affairs of men. It will normally be an unusual or unfamiliar event that does this to us: a dramatic recovery or escape, but it may also be a commonplace event like seeing a rainbow or an almond branch, which at that moment becomes wonderful and meaningful.

Whether a scientific explanation or description is available is neither here nor there. A fishery expert might explain the great draught of fishes (John 21: 4-8). A committee of doctors and psychiatrists could have given a report on the healing of the man born blind (John 9: 1), just as they have given many descriptions of the healings at Lourdes. They might be able to produce similar cures by their own techniques. But it is of the nature of a miracle that it demands to be described in a second language, in religious, personal language as well as in scientific language. The "extra" factor in a miracle is that suddenly we feel the opening up of a new dimension, a depth of mystery, and feel the presence of a personal element at work in nature, although nature usually seems impersonal.

Take an example: A healthy, middle-aged man is suddenly taken ill. His life is in danger and he does not respond to the usual treatments. His doctor in desperation tries a new drug and the man recovers. The man's wife talks about a miracle, the nurses talk about a miracle-drug, the doctor characteristically says nothing. The man thanks the doctor for his skill and care, and he is specially thankful for the new drug. He also feels grateful to God and begins to wonder whether his life has not been spared so that he can do some work that no one else could do. Was there a miracle? Was it the drug or the doctor or God who cured the patient?

First: Certainly God was at work. He is always at work. Whether God acted here through the doctor and the drug, or apart from them, or without them one can never know. All the doctor or the scientist can say is that in general, certain treatments produce certain results.

Second: Was there a miracle? Only if God's power was seen by the eye of faith at work in an extraordinary event. God may frequently act in a special way, but if no one sees and acknowledges it, it cannot be called a miracle. Again, God is as much at work in maintaining us in health from day to day as in saving us in crises, and we ought to give thanks for that, but because it is not extraordinary we do not call it a miracle.

Third: If the doctor, by studying this man's case, was able to use the drug to cure others, would that prove that the man's recovery had been no miracle? Not at all. The advance of science no more eliminates the possibility of miracle than it prevents us from believing in God. Indeed from one point of view the advance of science makes us more aware of the mystery of life and the limitations of our understanding. There was a time when a spade was just a spade, but nowadays the advance of science has shown something of the endless complexity of even the simplest things. The atomic and sub-atomic structure of the blade, the molecular structure of the wood will bring the most learned scientist to an awareness of the mystery which lies beyond the frontier of his knowledge.

It is perhaps the layman who is in greater danger, for he may begin to feel that everything is known, everything understood, and that everything operates by strictly determined laws, and begin to look at the world and himself as a collection of "things." In such a frame of mind belief not only in miracles, but also in God and in human responsibility would be in danger of fading away. However, science itself is not to be blamed for the misunderstandings of its admirers.

No doubt it was easier for the people of the Bible than it is for us to think of God as being active in nature and in history. They could see the hand of God or of demons almost directly behind *every* event.

We see long chains of cause and effect which can be followed back indefinitely. But in the end our situation is the same. Are we to interpret the events of life as mere events, the activity of demons or of mechanical causes, or do we believe that there is a God who over-rules all things?

If we believe in God we will expect to see signs which point to his power and his work.

It will always be possible for a skeptic to deny the reality of miracles. Whenever he hears someone claim that a miracle has occurred he will always be able to say that it was just an ordinary event about which some religious person got excited. If it is objected that no natural explanation can be found he can always reply that some day it will be found.

Against this, the Christian believer can do nothing, and should do nothing except to stick quietly to his story and to bear his witness. He can never expect the scientists either to prove or to disprove his miracle. Even a friendly scientist who believes in the miracle can say no more, as a scientist, than that no natural explanation is available, but he would always have to admit that one might be found some day. Miracles cannot be proved, they can only be testified to by faith, just as God's very existence cannot be scientifically proved but is always a confession of faith. All that can be seen with the outward eye is a natural happening. The Christian believes that God stands behind all natural events as Creator and Ruler of the universe, but he also believes that from time to time, in unexpected and novel ways, God will associate himself with some event, will act, will deal directly with some of his creatures. Directly, yet not quite directly, for even in miracles and even in revelation God remains a hidden God who can be seen only by the eye of faith. No man has seen God at any time: which is only to say that God is not a part of our physical universe, but its Creator and Lord. But God has acted and spoken. He has made himself known to men. And we believe that he still does. Miracles are outward signs of his action.

The story of Eddie Rickenbacker and his companions has become famous. When their plane went down in the Pacific Ocean the party drifted about for twenty-seven days in a rubber dinghy. Their supplies ran out and the chances of rescue seemed to have run out as well. One of the men had been reading aloud from his Bible when a seagull flew down and settled on Rickenbacker's head. To the castaways this was a sign. Capturing the bird they satisfied their hunger and thirst and waited with renewed hope the rescue which soon followed.

A natural explanation of this event can readily be made. Nevertheless for those men the experience was a miracle. For them it was a sign that God had not forsaken them. This sign, linked with the experience of being lost and saved, stirred them to the depths, and resulted in at least one of them going into full-time Christian work.

So miracle still occurs where there are eyes to see and faith to believe that God is present and active in his world.

Chapter 7

Man before God

*Man is created by God and designed
for a special relationship with him.
But he is unable to reach this goal
without divine help because of his sin.
His hope is in what God's love can do.*

To some questions like "What is two plus
two?" there is only one right answer. To others, like
"What is a Man?" many answers are right. A biologist
might say that a man is a male animal of the species
Homo sapiens, and a lawyer that a man is a male
over twenty-one, or a salesman that a man is a customer.
If we read that "the colonel posted a guard of a
sergeant and six men" we know that man here means
a private soldier. If we hear an outraged wife say to
her husband, "You're no man!", we know that men are
supposed to be distinguished by the virtues of strength
and courage. In different settings man is differently
described. In the Christian view what is it that makes
a man?

1. MAN: CREATED BY GOD

The first thing that the Bible says about man is that he is a *creature*: "God created man . . . male and female created he them" (Gen. 1: 27). What does this mean?

We will quite misunderstand it if we suppose that it is a question of man either being created by God or being descended from the apes. Man may be descended from the apes just as Joe Doakes may be descended from Sir Hezekiah Doakes who fought in the battle of Quebec. These are matters for the biologists or historians to look into. To say that man is God's creature is a different kind of statement, just as it is a different kind of statement again to say that man is a morally responsible agent. These different statements belong to different contexts (biological, historical, theological, and ethical) and may be true or false independently of one another.

What then does it mean theologically to say that man is a creature? It means that man is not alone, that he exists in the presence of God. He has not set and cannot set the terms of his own existence: they are set for him by God. He did not bring himself into existence, but on the other hand he was not merely thrown into existence. He is not the result of an evolutionary accident. Just as each of us is capable of meaningful and responsible behaviour, so our whole existence as men is a meaningful and responsible thing. *We have come into being by the will and in the purpose of God.* That gives us our dignity. But we will always be God's creatures and children, we are not ourselves God. If we try to become gods, to make ourselves the lords of our own life, we will not rise above the station that we have been given. We will fall below it.

Humanists, who believe there is nothing higher than man, accuse Christians of falling into two opposite errors. On the one hand, they say, we unduly exalt man by saying that God created him, thus giving him a dignity to which he is not entitled. Man, according to them, is simply the product of natural forces, the highest point so far reached by the evolutionary process. He is of no interest to any god, for the simple reason that gods are merely the product of human imagination.

The humanists accuse us, on the other hand, of robbing man of his proper dignity by suggesting that he is responsible to God who is his Lord and Judge as well as his Creator. They say that man is responsible only to himself, or to his own highest ideals, for there is nothing higher.

No one need deny that there is something noble about this picture of man. There is something pathetic about it too, for if it is true, man is the product of a purposeless and mindless process, he has nothing to be true to but himself. When he and the race die off that will be the end of it. And the stars in the lifeless heaven will shine on unaware that such a thing as man has ever been.

To say, as Christians do, that man is a creature is to accept for him a humbler place in the scheme of things but a far more meaningful one. It is God, not man, who is the centre of things, but this makes man's life more meaningful not less. Man is dependent on God for his being, his capacities and powers, and for

the gift of life that is daily renewed. Yet this gives
him a dignity he could not have for himself. No part
of man is divine, for his mind and soul no less than
his body are the work and the gift of God, but every
part of man has a dignity and a fitness of its own just
because it is God's gift.

2. Man: in the image of God

The same verse (Gen. 1: 27) which declares man
to be a creature makes a second affirmation about
him: that he was created "in the image of God." This
gives him a special dignity which singles him out from
other creatures. What "the image of God" really is
the Bible nowhere explains and Christian teachers have
had different suggestions to offer. Some have said that
it is human free will, others that it is reason, others
again that it is the powers of the soul, memory, understanding, and will. But what is basic to all these
suggestions and to the biblical story is that man is
made to live *in a special relationship* with God and
that it is the fellowship which he can have with God
which marks him out from the rest of creation. Man's
reason, his spirituality, his self-consciousness, his
capacity for entering into personal relationships of
trust and love, all these are the gifts that make man
capable of fellowship with God.

If you look at the way in which the word "image"
is used in the New Testament, you will see that it
has three main uses.

(*a*) It is used to signify man's distinctive humanity—
the meaning it has in the Old Testament (cf. James
3: 9).

(*b*) Second and more important: that Christ is the image of God (2 Cor. 4: 4; Col. 1: 15; Heb. 1: 3).

(*c*) The third use is to signify the likeness of God into which believers enter by faith (Col. 3: 10; 2 Cor. 3: 18; Rom. 8: 29).

The difference between the Old Testament and the New Testament uses of the word are significant. The New Testament seems to take a more pessimistic view of human nature. It is almost as if it were saying: "Yes, it is true that man was made in the image of God, but look what man has done to himself. He is no longer what God intended him to be. He has become a fallen man, a sub-man. Men as we know them today have fallen below the level of true human nature. If you want to see what a *true* man is really like, don't look at the men you see walking about the street, look at Jesus Christ. If you want to stop being a sub-man and become a real man you must be made over in the likeness of Christ. As you are, you are not really a man at all."

3. MAN: FALLEN

It may seem surprising to Christians that the New Testament should take a gloomier view of the state of human nature than the Old, but this seems to be true. For instance, the story of the fall of Adam in Genesis 3 is never mentioned in any other part of the Old Testament, but has a place of prominence in New Testament teaching and in the subsequent theology of the church. It is not that the Old Testament says little about sin. It says a great deal. But the New

Testament writers seem more alarmed about it. They treat it as a universal blight that has fallen on mankind. Not only some people, some of the time, but all the people all the time, are stricken with this deadly disease.

All this is related to the coming of Christ. In Jesus Christ the early Christians saw that human nature in the image of God was a far higher and nobler thing than they had ever imagined. By the same token we ourselves are in far worse condition than we had ever imagined. When we compare ourselves with other people we may seem good enough, even above average, but when we compare ourselves with Jesus Christ the bottom falls out of the pitcher of our self-esteem. His goodness judges us.

It is so even with ordinary good people. Just by being what they are their goodness is a standing reproach to the rest of us, and the greater the contrast the greater the reproach. We can respond to such people in two ways: we can accept them for what they are and send out our hearts to them in love and admiration and praise, but only if we accept ourselves for what we are, acknowledging our own weakness, or we can deny our own weakness and protect ourselves by denouncing them as false pretenders who put on an air of self-righteousness.

This is exactly what happened to Jesus. He attracted men strongly and he repelled men strongly. He roused the profoundest passions, the deepest loyalty and the deepest hatred. If the word of God divides like a two-edged sword, it can be said that *Jesus,* not only in the days of his flesh but *even now, divides men into those who confess him as Lord and those who cry out that he should be done away with.* If you keep your distance it is perhaps possible to be neutral, but if you come close you are in the presence of a judge; a strange judge indeed who makes men pass sentence on him, but who makes us judge ourselves in judging him.

It is no accident that it was the publicans and sinners who found it easy to like Jesus and to accept him. They knew they were no good. He did not upset their good opinion of themselves, for they had no such opinion. It was precisely those who felt that they had some moral and religious accomplishments in which to take pride who found it hardest to accept Jesus and easiest to reject him.

In Jesus Christ we see what man is really like. In him we see the true dignity and the full stature of human nature in the image of God. More than that, by being what he was he brings out both the best and the worst in other people. He brings out the worst in human nature so that men in desperate self-defence and self-justification turn against him and show how depraved they can be. He brings out the best in human nature when men in contrition and love give themselves to him that they may be remade in his likeness.

Christians are sometimes accused (inconsistently perhaps) of two opposite faults: of being cynical about human nature when they emphasize sin and of being sentimental about it when they speak of the glorious destiny that is opened up for man in Christ. In fact the boot is on the other foot, for it is precisely Christians who can be saved from both these faults.

People with a shallow view of human nature, who do not know what is in man (John 2: 25), are likely to have a cosy and sentimental idea of what men are like, and when that is shaken by some experience of human wickedness are likely to be plunged into despair and bitterness and become cynics. Or else, because a full-blown cynicism demands a greater strength of character than most people possess, they will be sentimental about themselves and their friends, and cynical about their enemies. Sentimentality and cynicism belong together and people with a shallow view of human nature oscillate between the two.

Those who know Jesus Christ, and have read the gospel story with understanding can be saved from this. They know the depth of human depravity, for they have seen it in the crucifixion. They know that this evil is in their own hearts. No new disclosure of men's weakness can surprise them, but neither can it make them lose their faith and their hope and their love for men. In Jesus Christ they have seen disclosed a new resource. They can despair of no one for whom Christ has given himself. They are ashamed of themselves, but they are proud of God's love for them, and God's love is not for them alone but for all sinners.

PART TWO

Jesus Christ and the Christian Life

ΕΓΕΝΕΤΟΔΕΕΝΤΑΙ
ΗΜΕΡΑΙΣΕΚ ΝΑΙΝ
ΕΞΗΛΘΕΝΛΟ ΜΑ
ΠΑΡΑΚΑΙΣΑ ΟΣΑ
ΓΟΥΣΤΟΥΑΠΟΓΡΑ
ΦΕΣΘΕΠΑΣΑΝΤΙΝ
ΟΙΚΟΥΜΕΝΗΝΛΥ
ΤΗΝΑΠΟΓΡΑΦΗΝ
ΕΤΕΝΕΤΟΠΡΩΤΗ
ΗΤΕΜΟΕΥΟΝΤ
ΤΗΣΣΥΡΙΑΣΚΥΡΗΝΙ
ΟΥΚΑΙΕΠΟΡΕΥΟΝ
ΤΟΕΚΑΣΤΟΣΑΠΟΓΡΑ

Chapter 8

The Bible and the Word of God

*Why Jesus wrote nothing. The Word
of God is not a book: it is God
giving us himself. So our faith is in
Christ, not in words. And the value of
the Bible is that it bears witness to him.*

Why did Jesus not write a book? This
question used to occur to me when I was in Sunday
school, and so far as I know none of my teachers
ever answered it. It is a question worth asking just
the same. Why didn't he write a book and give the
answer once and for all to the many questions we
would like to ask? Just think how many controversies
would have been avoided if Jesus had put down in
clear and orderly fashion the answers to these questions
about which Christians have argued. Should Christians
take part in war? Is the pope infallible? Is divorce
ever permitted? Should infants be baptized? Just
think of all the trouble the church would have been

spared if Jesus had given clear and final answers in a book.

But he didn't. He wrote nothing.

The fragments of his teaching that have been handed down to us are of priceless value, but they are a long way from being a complete guide to faith and morals. It almost looks as if Jesus quite deliberately decided that we were not to have such a thing.

He left behind him no book: *instead he left behind a community* of men who were to go out and build the church. They wrote a book—the New Testament—but even it is far from being a well-planned textbook and much of it (for instance Paul's letters) was written for special congregations and not for the church as a whole. He expected them to be read a few times, not permanently in the church.

If you think this strange—it becomes even stranger when you compare it with another religion: Islam. The prophet Mohammed who founded Islam wrote its holy book, the Koran, from beginning to end. When he was asked whether he could perform miracles he pointed to the Koran and said, "That is my miracle. I brought that book down from heaven." He claimed that every word in the Koran was given to him by God in dreams and trances and that every word was infallibly inspired.

What a contrast! The prophet Mohammed presents a book to his community with the claim that every word is from God. Jesus leaves no book. His community writes many books: the Gospels of Matthew, Mark, Luke, and John, Andrew, Peter, Philip, and

Thomas, and then it argues for years as to which of them are to be authorized for official use in the church. They accept some and reject others. The contrast is almost absolute. The Koran was written from beginning to end by one man who claimed it was all given by God. The New Testament is many books written by many men over many years, edited and argued over by the church community. Most of them make no claim to ecstatic inspiration, but were written in a quite simple and practical way as letters to young churches. Doesn't it look as if the Koran has a far better claim to be the word of God than the New Testament has? And if, instead of talking about the New Testament, you take *the Bible* as a whole, you find that it *was written over many centuries* and has a long complex history of editing. What does this all mean?

1. WHAT THE WORD OF GOD IS

One thing it means is that *Christians don't mean the same thing by "the word of God" that Muslims do.* For Mohammed the word of God was a book and he was the prophet who brought the book. For Christians the word of God is (in the last instance) a man: Jesus, who was called the Christ. In Islam the man points to the book. In Christianity the book points to the man. Many people think Islam is a much simpler religion than Christianity and perhaps it is. But that doesn't make it truer: we have to take Christianity for what it is, and one thing that this contrast with Islam shows us is that the heart and centre of the Christian message is not about a sacred book which a prophet brings down from heaven, but about a man in whom God comes to meet us and to whom the church in its writings and in its life bears witness.

When you read in Jeremiah "The word of the Lord came unto me saying . . ." you don't get the impression that Jeremiah was a secretary writing things down. You get the impression that he was a man brought face to face with God, being sent to go and *do* something, to go and *be* something. Jeremiah wasn't like a telegraph boy touching his cap and taking a message for delivery. He is a man on fire about the injustice of the world and the sins of his people and the holiness of God, driven out to plead and to threaten and to fight. *When Jeremiah says, "the word of the Lord came to me,"* he is not talking about being given some words of wisdom to pass on, but about coming face to face with holiness and justice and majesty, about being shaken in his shoes by seeing the truth. *He is talking about encountering God himself.*

When the Gospel of John calls Jesus Christ the Word of God it means that in Jesus Christ men were brought face to face with God. He didn't come to hand over a message about God, not even a message from God. The early Christians believed that something far more wonderful than that has happened. They believed that, in Jesus, God himself had come to meet them.

The word of God means a lot more than words about God, it means God himself come face to face with men. This is true for the Old Testament prophet when the word of God comes to him. It is true about Jesus Christ, the Word of God incarnate. It is even true about preaching, which we call the ministry of the word because in preaching it is expected that we will be brought face to face with the majesty of God and with his power.

We live in an age when words seem to have lost their value. The newspapers print thousands and millions of words every day and we have learned to distrust many of them. The radio announcers rattle off 150 words a minute about somebody's soap and somebody else's finance company and we learn to listen with only half an ear. As we travel about the big cities we are always in the midst of voices talking, shouting, laughing, protesting, all bombarding us with words so that we have to learn how to shut off our hearing and draw back to be alone with ourselves.

Why do words degenerate till they become just noises in the air or marks on paper? Why do we sometimes toss the newspaper away or switch the radio off with a feeling of despair at the emptiness of all these words? Isn't the thing that gets us down the fact that they are *just* words, that there is nobody behind them? They are empty because they are impersonal. We'd rather have one real word spoken to our face by a living being than all the rest of these empty noises and empty marks. One living word spoken to us, even in anger, so long as it was spoken *to* us, would be real: and it would be real because it's personal, there is somebody behind it.

Did you ever think what it means when one person says to another, "I give you my word"? They stand up and they look solemnly at one another, their eyes meet and their hands touch. "I give you my word." What are they doing? They are making a covenant

with one another, a personal undertaking, a commitment. "I give you my word" almost means "I give you
myself."

It is in this way that we should think of the word
of God. It is always something personal. It is God
facing man, making a bond, not giving out a piece of
information but coming himself into the life of someone. When the word of the Lord came to the prophet
Jeremiah—or any of the prophets—it wasn't that God
gave him some information about the future which he
might pass on to others, but that God himself came into
this man's life, to change it, making him a new man
doing new things.

Put it another way: what happens in Revelation?
Does God reveal things about the future, about the
furniture of heaven and the temperature of hell? Does
he impart messages to people to be recorded and passed
on? This is secondary. Revelation is always something
personal. When John gives Mary his word, he isn't
giving her a new piece of information she didn't have
before, he is giving her himself. When God's word
comes to man, God is giving man himself. What he
reveals is not something but someone: himself. That
is why we talk about the word of God rather than the
words of God. God might tell us numberless things
about the universe that we don't know and can't find
out and these might all be words from God. But the
word of God is only *one* thing and it is always the same:
God's own nature and being and character made clear
to us. When God gives us his word, he gives us himself.

This then is why the word of God is more than a
book, more even than the most precious of all books.

To read about somebody is important and useful, but it is not like *knowing* him. To have information about somebody is fine, but to have his friendship is so different as hardly to be comparable. So the revelation of God can never be merely something written in a book; it must be always a meeting with a person. We call the Bible the word of God because it tells us about meetings with God, about how God has encountered men in their lives, and because through this book we also can encounter God. We call Jesus Christ the Word of God because if God is personal we can never know him adequately in a book or in a doctrine, but only in a person who is flesh and blood.

The Bible is like a telescope: it is for looking through, not looking at. It is not itself revealed, it is the witness to revelation, the record of revelation, it is the testimony of the church that God has revealed himself to his people, to the prophets, to the apostles but most of all *in* Jesus Christ.

Why didn't Jesus write a book? To save us from a false view of faith and from a false view of inspiration.

2. WHAT FAITH IS

Jesus spent much of his time fighting against the Pharisees and said some surprisingly bitter things about them. This is strange, for the Pharisees were far from being irreligious people. They were indeed the strongest and most vigorous group in the Jewish religious scene. Why was Jesus so strongly against them? Partly at least because they had turned the worship of the living God into a religion of a book. They had taken the Old Testament and made it into a set of rules governing

every detail of life. Obey the rules and you were saved;
disobey them and you were lost. It was a nice cut and
dried religion. You knew where you were. You could
add up your moral score card at the end of the day and
see exactly where you stood, or thought you stood.

Apparently Jesus believed that this sort of religion
makes men hard-hearted bigots. He wanted a personal
religion not a legal one. He wanted men to have a
personal relationship with God, one of trust and
obedience. He seems to have believed that if you
had the right relationship with God you didn't need
a book of moral rules, you could be trusted to "play
it by ear."

Isn't that why he told simple stories when he taught
the people? Isn't that why he taught in parables instead
of revising the law books of the Pharisees? Isn't that
why he did not write a book but let people learn from
what he did and from what he was? Of course we need
laws and we need books and we need doctrines, but
they come second. Jesus left it to the church to provide
them so that they might always stand second to what
he was and what he did. Christian faith doesn't really
mean believing the *things* that you read in the Bible:
it means believing in the God that the Bible tells you
about, trusting him and obeying him.

3. WHAT INSPIRATION IS

This is a much more complex question and we must
take it step by step. Some people say the Bible is
inspired because it is inspiring. Many passages in the
Bible are indeed inspiring. You can't listen to the

fortieth chapter of Isaiah or the thirteenth of First Corinthians without feeling that this is great literature. But there is other great literature in the world that is also inspiring: speeches from Shakespeare, sonnets by Milton, and so on. Plenty of passages in the Bible aren't inspiring at all, in the book of Leviticus for instance. There are many sections of the Bible that are just dull to most people and there is no reason why we should deny it. It is not necessary to claim that the Bible is great literature from one end to the other, and even if you did that would no more make it the word of God than *Hamlet* or *Paradise Lost*.

Then many people say that the Bible is the word of God because it is infallible: every word in it is unconditionally true. This is an ancient view and since it has caused great trouble in the church we need to look at it honestly and carefully. The argument is put forward in many ways. Here is one:

> The Bible was written by men, but these men were directed by God, so God is its final author. God cannot err so the scriptures cannot err. Nobody has ever proved the scriptures to be wrong at any point. Where they appear to conflict with science, for instance, then either science is wrong or we haven't been interpreting the scriptures properly.

Two things must be said about this:

(*a*) If someone wishes to claim that the scriptures are infallible he can never be proved wrong. If it is claimed for instance that the Bible teaches that the world was created in six days, around 4000 B.C., or that the world is flat and the sky an inverted bowl and that modern science contradicts this, the believer in biblical infallibility has a double answer: First, only the original text of scripture is infallible and we cannot tell what errors may have crept in over the centuries, and second, though the text of scripture is infallible we may be interpreting it wrongly. So no apparent conflict between the Bible and science ought ever to be taken as evidence against the theory that the Bible is infallible. This is fine for the theory, but it means that the Bible is only infallible in an original text which we do not have, and in an interpretation which we do not know.

(*b*) The claim of infallibility does not in fact add up to much unless someone claims to have an infallible interpretation of the infallible book, and this is the second point. The Roman Catholics quite rightly see that if you are to have a doctrine of infallibility you must go the whole way and have an infallible pope. What would be the use of God giving us an infallible Bible if fifty different people are going to give fifty different interpretations of it? If it is infallibility you want, you need an infallible church, too. Without that it may be emotionally comforting to claim that God caused the Bible to be composed without error but it is useless to those who cannot guarantee to interpret it without error.

Our concern need not be to attack the doctrine of infallibility. It is far more important to point to a true doctrine of inspiration. I believe one reason why Jesus did not write a book is that he wishes to guard us against the error of worshipping a book when we should be worshipping God.

We can find the way to a true doctrine of the Bible

as the word of God by following Luther and Calvin. This may come as a surprise, for many people think that the infallibility of scripture is the Reformation position. In the form in which we have it today, this doctrine did not grow up till some time after the Reformation. Luther himself, unquestionably one of the greatest biblical scholars, once said that he would not waste his time arguing with people who did not believe that the scriptures are the word of God. But he also taught that what made the scriptures the word of God was their witness to Christ. The scriptures can err in mundane things, in matters of science for instance. Where they are right is where they point to Christ. Said Luther:

> Christ is the Lord and King of the scriptures. . . . All sound books agree in this, that they witness to Christ. That is the proper test by which to judge all books, whether they preach Christ. . . . That which does not preach Christ is not apostolic though it came from St. Peter or St. Paul. Contrariwise that which preaches Christ would be apostolic even though it came from Judas or Annas or Pilate or Herod.

That is the first point: scripture is not the word of God because of any mechanical theory of infallibility, but because it is the witness to God as he has revealed himself to men. But now the second point: Luther wrote:

> Not only have these things happened (not only has God spoken to men, revealed himself to them) and not only does the Bible proclaim this, but the Holy Ghost also writes it inwardly in our hearts.

This was the aspect of Luther's teaching that Calvin took up. Calvin showed that there are all kinds of ways of trying to prove that the Bible is the word of God by argument. You can point to the eloquence of scripture, but that only proves what good writers the prophets and apostles were. You can try to show that the Bible has never been contradicted by later historical research, but that would only prove that the biblical writers were good historians. You can try to show that the Bible never contradicts modern science, but that would only prove that the Hebrew scientists were away ahead of their time. No, says Calvin, none of these arguments is enough. If we are to be persuaded of what we really want to know—Is God in this, or is it just the imaginations of men?—then God must bear witness to himself. This is Calvin's famous doctrine of the inner testimony of the Holy Spirit. God bears witness to himself, it is he who gives us the assurance that we look for and it is only he who could do it.

Not only is the Bible an authentic reliable record of God's encounters with men in the past, but God uses it to speak to men in the present.

4. WHAT THEN IS THE AUTHORITY OF THE BIBLE?

First of all, *the Bible is the book about Jesus Christ*: about his life and ministry and teaching, his death and resurrection, and about the community that he sent out into the world. And since you must know the background, the Christian church put the whole of the Old Testament into the Bible believing that it is all a preparation for Christ and leads up to him.

Secondly, the Bible has at least the authority of *an authentic record*, maybe not infallible in all its details but certainly authentic. When the early church chose out of the many books that were circulating these four Gospels, these letters of Paul and James and John and Peter, this Apocalypse, it was testifying that these books are reliable. Not that the church was giving them their authority, it was giving official recognition to the fact that these books have authority in themselves.

Thirdly, *the books of the Bible* do not argue nor seek to prove. They testify and *bear witness* that there is a God, that he has acted in the lives of men, and that in Jesus Christ he has come in the flesh. John says:

> . . . the life was made manifest, and we saw it, and testify to it, and proclaim to you the eternal life which was with the Father and was made manifest to us . . . (1 John 1: 2).

The biblical writers are saying, "A word has come from God, hear it."

Fourthly, when the minister reads the scriptures in church and says, "Hear the word of God," he is not just saying hear the words of this book, he is saying, "This has been a word from God, hear it." And he says this because the church has confidence that as God has borne witness to himself in the past so *he will bear witness to himself in the present*. It happens! The Bible *does* come alive and those who know this can only say, "It is true, God does speak through this book. And when he speaks, you must respond by believing in him, by obeying him, by following him." And if people ask you why you do this you can only say, "Because God has spoken and I have heard."

Chapter 9

The Incarnate God

First-hand religion begins as an encounter. In Jesus we see human greatness, but he is more than a great man, and we must decide for or against him as divine.

When Paul Levertoff died in London, many regarded him as something of a saint. He was born in Russia, and born a Jew. His family intended that he should become a rabbi and he began to study for that end. One day in a public park in the city a passing stranger slipped into his hand a copy of the Gospel according to John. The young man sat down to read the book and rose up a Christian believer.

There are, I am sure, many ways of becoming a Christian, but there seems to me to be something peculiarly satisfactory about *that* way. Most of us grow up in Christian homes, we hear the Bible stories from our parents, we are taken to Sunday school, we sing

Christian hymns, we take in Christianity as it were through our pores, from a Christian society all round about us. It is a very wonderful thing to grow up in a Christian family, a Christian country, and the Christian church, but it can be confusing. It can lead us to take Christianity very much for granted, so that we never really know what it means to decide for or against it. It can lead us to accept, or reject, Christianity for reasons which may be quite irrelevant.

Some people have rejected Christ for equally trivial reasons which is a pity. It is also a pity when people *accept* Christianity for poor or insufficient reasons. It is good when people are drawn to Christianity by love of their parents or respect for their minister or by associating Christianity with good works and good fellowship. *It is bad if these things become a substitute for a real encounter with Jesus Christ himself.* So often they do. How much better to meet Christ himself head on, for instance by reading a penny copy of a Gospel slipped into your hand by a stranger.

Suppose we are orthodox enough in our beliefs. We could give the right answers about Christianity. And we would believe the answers we give. Still, probably few of us are orthodox in our imaginations (as Auden said of Charles Williams) so that we naturally and inevitably think in a Christian way and with a Christian instinct. I have the impression that those who can do this are often people who have come to Christ from outside, either because they were brought up in some other faith, or because they lapsed from the Christianity of their childhood and returned.

Is it not significant that several of the best known of our Christian writers and poets, who have to have

Christian imaginations, and cannot just spout opinions they have learned, are people who have come *back* to Christianity later in life? Think of T. S. Eliot, W. H. Auden, C. S. Lewis. There is a freshness and sureness of touch about such people which the majority of us do not have.

How can we have if, to speak for a moment in paradoxes, we had the bad luck to be brought up in a Christian home and a Christian congregation?

1. A PERSONAL ENCOUNTER WITH JESUS CHRIST

How can Christian faith be renewed in those who get it second hand?

I suggest that we may do so, *not by a course of lectures in doctrine but by a personal encounter with Jesus Christ.* This is how Christianity started in the first place. And this how it has always been renewed in each generation.

When you listen to people talking about Christian faith, as I have been doing in these pages, you might well get the impression that Christianity is a set of ideas, of doctrines, rather like physics or chemistry, and that to be a Christian you must believe a, b, c, d, . . . and so many other things or ideas or doctrines about God, man, and the universe.

This is a mistake.

Christian belief certainly involves large numbers of specific doctrines. Many people like myself spend a great deal of time arguing about particular points of doctrine and we always run the risk of giving the impression that the doctrine itself is the real thing. But it is not. Doctrine is always secondary. Doctrine is only the attempt to interpret and to set forth in careful words the primary experience itself. *Christianity is not a system of doctrine delivered to us by Jesus Christ. It is first of all belief in Jesus Christ himself*, and *then* it is *a system of teaching* worked out by believers to express what they have learned about God, man and human life from Jesus Christ.

Two hundred years ago it was customary to speak and to think of Jesus as "the founder of Christianity," just as Gautama the Buddha was the founder of Buddhism and Mohammed was the founder of Islam. People spoke of each of them as though they had all done essentially the same thing. They lived among men and left behind their distinctive teachings. If that were the main truth then the teaching would be the primary and important thing and the teacher secondary. Most Buddhists and all Muslims would agree that this is so. They revere the founder, but they believe the teachings. Is this also true for Christianity?

You remember the story of the minister who used to exhort his people from the pulpit and end up by saying, "Don't do as I do, do as I tell you." A minister ought to be an example to his people, but no one expects him to be a perfect example. No right-minded Christian supposes that because the minister has certain faults the congregation are thereby authorized to have the same faults. If a minister exemplifies the gospel he preaches so much the better, but we listen to him for the gospel itself, not for what he is. That is why he is called a minister, a servant, of the gospel he preaches.

Mohammed could also say, "Don't do as I do, do as I tell you." Mohammed claimed to be only a messenger of God. There are things about Mohammed's life that are not wholly admirable, but that would not disturb an intelligent Muslim any more than it should disturb us to observe weaknesses in the character of Paul or Jeremiah. Muslims do not believe in Mohammed but in the Koran. It is the Koran which is the revelation of God, and Islam is a religion of a book.

There are people who treat Christianity as though it were a religion of a book, too. But remember, although we allow ourselves to talk about the Bible as the word of God, we do not say this as a Muslim would say it about the Koran. For them the Koran is the word of God and Mohammed is the prophet through whom that word came. He points to the book. For us Jesus Christ is the Word of God, and the Bible is the witness to the Word. The book points to Christ.

What I want to say could be put in three statements:

— Christianity does not claim to be a collection of human teachings but a divine revelation.
— What God is supposed to have revealed is not a set of doctrines but his own nature, himself.
— God made this revelation of himself in a person, Jesus of Nazareth.

Buddhists revere Buddha because he was a great teacher and they follow his teaching and believe that his teachings lead to salvation. Muslims r e v e r e Mohammed because it was through him that the Koran came and they believe the Koran to be the word of God. Christians worship Jesus of Nazareth, and call him the Christ because they believe that *he himself* was the revelation of God.

Historians can look at Christianity and say that here

Christianity has had a good effect on our civilization and there it has had a bad effect. Philosophers can look at this or that piece of Christian doctrine and say that it is good or bad. Psychologists can say that various Christian beliefs and practices are helpful or harmful to our psychic states. They can all look at other religions and say the same things, but none of these observations will tell us whether Christianity is true or false. To be told that the command to love your neighbour is morally sound, or psychologically helpful, or the basis of sociological security is interesting. But it does not answer the question, "What do you think of the Christ, whose Son is he?" And it is by the answer to that question that Christianity stands or falls.

We can all go through life accepting Christianity because it is expected of us, or because other people whom we respect are Christians, or because Christianity makes people sleep better or makes them socially acceptable or is the answer to communism. That will always be Christianity at second hand. If we are to have the real thing, if our faith is not to be a load on our back, but wings, we must answer the question for ourselves, "What do you think of the Christ?"

2. The greatness of Jesus' character

We probably have a better chance of answering that question than any generation since Jesus' own time. We have access to modern translations of the scriptures, to commentaries on them from all points of view, to background materials and comparative studies in abundance. And what do they tell us?

This to begin with, that by any standards Jesus must

have been a very remarkable man. Considering that he left behind him no written records, that we are wholly dependent for our knowledge upon books written by plain men without any special skill as journalists, the picture of Jesus that comes to us in the Gospels is amazingly clear and consistent. It can only be explained by the presumption that *Jesus made a remarkably vivid impression on those who heard him.*

(*a*) One reason for this is that he was unquestionably *a poet.* All of us can have deep experiences; many of us have a fairly shrewd insight, but it takes a poet to express these things neatly, memorably, and beautifully so that men carry the saying about with them in their minds. The Gospels are full of these sayings which he seems to have flung off easily and yet with perfect assurance:

> Consider the lilies of the field, how they grow;
>   they toil not, neither do they spin:
> And yet I say unto you, That even Solomon in all
>   his glory was not arrayed like one of these.

(*b*) A second reason is that he was unquestionably a great *philosopher.* Nowadays the word philosopher is sometimes used to refer to people who spend their time on abstract problems, full of ingenuity but rather useless. Originally a philosopher was a lover of wisdom, a man who was not just clever, or learned, or ingenious, but *wise.* And such a one Jesus certainly was. Time and time again you see him in the Gospels going to the heart of a moral situation, never taking refuge in obscurity, never using a long word to cover up a vague thought, but expressing the deepest truths in the simplest words. Just think of the stories of the good

Samaritan or the prodigal son. What could be simpler
and what more profound?

(*c*) A third reason why Jesus impressed people was
that this simplicity was no cover-up for weakness of
intellect. He was without question *brilliant and fearless
in his thought.* The impression of relaxed ease and
friendliness which he gives us should not allow us to
forget that all his ministry he was being watched and
spied on and that traps were being constantly set for
him by his enemies. Think of the brilliant passage of
wits recorded in Matthew 21: 23 ff. Jesus is challenged
to say whether he believes himself to have authority
from God. It is the question we all want to ask. But
Jesus will not answer, not only because to say yes would
have landed him in jail, but because it would have
prevented the simple response of faith to himself and
his teaching which he was always working for. So he
parries with another question, "The baptism of John,
was it from heaven or from men?" His accusers cannot
answer, for if they say, "From heaven," Jesus will reply,
"Then why did you not follow him?" If they say, "From
men," they will convict themselves of spiritual blindness
in the eyes of the people. Jesus in the most brilliant
way has shown that their question was a dishonest one.
Could any lawyer have turned the problem more
neatly?

(*d*) A fourth reason why Jesus impressed people was
his *courage.* Most men would rather have courage
than any other virtue and Jesus evidently had it to a
supreme degree: not the down-beating kind of courage
which covers up an inner uncertainty, but the real kind

which is compatible with gentleness. To me the most impressive thing about Jesus' career is his unswerving self-control as he faces the cross. Not only could he have escaped death up to the last moment (he could easily have slipped off and ended his days quietly in the country), but he could easily have broken down under the strain. Yet there is no evidence of anything like that. To the very end it is Jesus who is in perfect control and everyone else who falters and loses nerve; the disciples, the high priests, Pilate, Herod: all of them vacillate and make false moves, but not Jesus.

Quite apart from any judgment of faith, anyone who reads the story has to admit that here was a man of superb intelligence, flawless character, deep sympathies and unfaltering courage. That is the positive side, and about it all men seem to agree.

Hindus and Buddhists, Muslims and Jews, atheists and humanists, have united in their admiration of Jesus and his teachings. You will find statues of Jesus in Hindu temples, side by side with statues of Krishna and Vishnu. There were paintings of Jesus in the temple at Mecca in Mohammed's day. Communist orators will still refer to Comrade Jesus as one who would have had his party card had he been alive today.

3. JESUS CHRIST IS MORE THAN A GREAT MAN

But there is another side. Not only is Jesus one whom men and women of all ages and nations and creeds unite to praise: *He is also the most controversial figure in human history.*

His followers, who knew him best and upon whom we are dependent for all our historical knowledge of

him, say that on the third day after he was buried he
rose again from the dead, and that he continued to
appear to them from time to time until he was "taken
up into heaven." They recorded many wonderful
healings and unusual deeds. Some of them we can
explain, some of them we cannot. But the point of
them as far as the disciples were concerned was this:
they were signs that Jesus had been given a special
authority by God and was indeed bringing in the
kingdom of God, of which these miracles were the
first fruits. Again, when his followers recorded many
of his stories and sayings they implied that Jesus, in
teaching and doing these things, was claiming a special
authority from God.

Finally, the followers of Jesus said that he was no
ordinary teacher or prophet, but one especially sent by
God. He was something like the Messiah who had been
expected by the Jews, but even more than that. They
called him, from the very earliest times, Lord and
Christ. "Believe," they said, "on the Lord Jesus Christ."
In saying so they were summing up all that was later
developed in orthodox Christianity. They were saying
that Jesus Christ was divine.

What are we to make of that? Were the disciples
of Jesus just ignorant peasants who misunderstood?
They were not educated men by our standards, but
they were not fools. They probably had as much intelligence as you or I, perhaps more. Not only that, they
were all strict Jews, pledged to fight idolatry and to
defend monotheism to the death. For such men to call
Jesus Lord is indeed startling. What are we to say?

All kinds of attempts have been made to solve the problem:

— accept the teaching of Jesus but not the teaching about Jesus? But the Messianic claims are so woven into the teaching that they cannot be separated.

— accept the simple teaching of the gospels but reject the elaborate theology of Paul? But the gospels themselves express all the great orthodox claims.

— separate the New Testament from the later development of orthodox doctrine in the church? But the roots of orthodoxy are already to be found in the New Testament and cannot be avoided.

Do not think that the Christian church came easily to write its creeds and to make its claims. All the objections to orthodoxy that you or I have ever thought of were thought of in the first three centuries, and many more that have not occurred to us. Spend a day reading the literature of the great church debates of the fourth century and you will quickly shed the idea that the creeds were written by credulous and simple-minded people who wanted to make things mysterious and didn't know how to argue.

The facts of the case forced orthodox Christianity upon the church, and I do not really believe that anything very different could have been said. We might vary the wording and change the expressions, but the great creeds are hard to avoid, given the New Testament.

During his career in Palestine, Jesus forced his enemies into a corner. They had either to accept him and his claims or kill him. He has been doing the same to men ever since. I myself believe that there are only two responses you can make to Jesus. Either you say as Christian orthodoxy has always said, "My Lord and my God!" Or you wash your hands like Pilate and acknowledge that you do not know what to make of such a combination of the impressive and the incredible.

There is an ancient saying: *Aut Deus, aut non bonus homo.* Either he was God, or he was not even a good man, a deceiver who deliberately used his amazing abilities to mislead millions of people. Which is the harder to believe? If he was a wicked man he must have been wicked with a quite diabolical wickedness to have assumed such an appearance of goodness, more than that, to have given the impression of being good through and through. And that so much inspiration and spiritual power should have come from a hidden wickedness is hard to believe.

But how hard *is* it to believe that he is God? To believe it in cold blood, as an exercise in credulity, to accept it as authority because someone you respect tells you to believe it: that would be not only hard but wrong. If it is said because you think it is the right thing to say, or because people expect it, it will be nothing but a burden, a load of dead orthodoxy on your back, it will trouble your conscience and sap your energies.

But if you say it as the disciples of old said it, because, having met Jesus and journeyed with him, you can only confess in amazement and adoration, "You are the Christ, the Son of the living God," then all will be different. Then this will not be *one more* doctrine to be believed, but something which explains all the rest.

I have spoken of different aspects of the nature and work of God as Christians understand it. I have said that he is Creator, that he is a loving Father, that his providential care is with us in all our sufferings and that it is his grace that empowers us for good. Some may think that so much is reasonable, but that to believe in the Incarnation, in God coming to us as a man, is unreasonable, something beyond belief. Yes it is beyond belief in the sense that no one, certainly no Jew, could ever have imagined this for himself. Those who came to believe it said it was in no sense a belief they had just come to like and to accept. It was something forced on them by the facts. What made them feel it was true was that, given this, everything fell into place. If God was like Jesus, of course he is a loving Father, a faithful and gracious Lord—just like Jesus. To believe in Jesus Christ is not to add one more burden of belief, but to be able to abandon all the doctrines as doctrines and see them simply as facts.

Thomas à Kempis said once, "The Holy Ghost had delivered me from a multitude of opinions." So all the followers of Jesus should be able to say: We have only one opinion, so much more than an opinion, that Jesus Christ is Lord. The rest follows naturally. We no longer really believe in doctrine at all. We believe in God, who came among us and taught and died and rose again for our salvation. We no longer have merely orthodox beliefs—we are being remade in the image of him who first made us.

Chapter 10

The Atonement

*The cross is at the heart of Christianity
though no theory about it has satisfied
the church. By his sacrifice Jesus has
delivered from sin's power those who
trust him, making them at one with God.
In this we see God's plan and act.*

If there is one thing that can be said to be
the centre of Christian belief and Christian worship it
is the conviction that Jesus Christ lived and died to
save men from their sins. The New Testament is shot
through and through with this conviction.

1. THE CROSS IS CENTRAL

The hymns of the church in all ages make this their
favourite subject. Almost every type of Christian seems
to rejoice in this aspect of the faith, whether it be the
Pentecostalist talking about being washed in the blood,
or the Roman Catholic focusing his devotions on the
crucifix or on the mass. To be sure there are other

things besides this and from time to time worthy
Christians protest that our emphasis on the death of
Christ should not lead us to forget his birth or his
resurrection or ascension or his life and teaching. Still,
it is the cross rather than the manger or the empty tomb
or the sermon on the mount which has been the focus
of Christian life. It is the cross which has become the
symbol of Christianity the world over. In the judgment
of the ages it is the cross that best leads us to the living
heart of Christianity. To read from the Gospels the
story of Jesus dying for us seems to be the simplest way
of telling people what Christianity is about. This speaks
directly, so that the simplest Christian understands at
once and is moved and his heart goes out to his Lord in
an answering love and obedience.

Theologians argue endlessly about the meaning of
the cross without ever reaching an entirely satisfactory
way of explaining how the death of Jesus could save
us from our sins. Faithful Christians have never been
unduly troubled by these failures. The early councils
of the church made statements about the *person*
of Christ which became touchstones of orthodoxy.
Strangely enough, no such official statement has ever
been made to interpret the *death* of Christ. The cross
itself has always held the hearts of faithful Christians,
though no one theory about the cross has ever held
the mind of the church.

This is a very good thing. It was not by theories
that God was pleased to save his people but by his
well-beloved Son. It is Christ himself not theories about
him that matter. Forgiveness, salvation, atonement,
reconciliation—these are personal things and if we are

to have them we must come into a new personal relationship with God. No theories will take the place of that.

Nobody can have his sins forgiven by reading a book. He has to be forgiven by God and accept that forgiveness. No one can experience reconciliation by being told about it. He has to be reconciled. No one is cured of a disease by reading in a medical text book what the right treatment is. No one who has quarreled with a friend improves things by knowing how the quarrel might be made up. He must go to the friend and do these things and have them responded to, or else the friend must come to him and he must respond. As long as they just sit and think about it the break between them remains. Something must be done. So it is between God and men.

Because of all this it is not a bad thing that none of our theories about the cross are finally satisfactory, and it is understandable and very moving that when, as common sinners who know the longing for forgiveness, we look at the cross, we know in our hearts what this is all about. We know the hopelessness and frustration that comes from falling out with a friend and how much it costs to restore a friendship. We know the loneliness and the guilt, the pride and stubborness, the resentment and bitterness that come with even trivial quarrels. It is when we are in the wrong that we show the worst side of our natures and are most unreasonable. We know how difficult it is to accept forgiveness, for it means admitting that we are in the wrong and need to be forgiven. We know how we snarl at any one who tries to help us, for we want to be left alone in our

misery and resist any approach to our loneliness. Like
the demon-possessed man who cried out when he saw
Jesus, "What have you to do with me . . . do not torment
me" (Mark 5: 7), we fear and hate the one who comes
to save us. When we look at the cross we see all this:
the vicious anger of the sinner that lashes out at the
one who comes to bring forgiveness, and the cost of
reconciliation.

2. WHAT WE CANNOT DO FOR OURSELVES

One of the first and most important things that Christians have always said about the work of Christ is that
it is something we could never have done for ourselves.
"Death is swallowed up in victory," wrote Paul, ". . .
thanks be to God, who gives us the victory through our
Lord Jesus Christ" (1 Cor. 15: 54, 57). In all ages of
the church, people have echoed that cry, saying that
without Christ they would have been lost, but he has
opened up the gates of a new life. For Christians Jesus
is more than a teacher, more even than a leader, he is
a Saviour. To be sure, in his parables and sayings he is
an unrivalled teacher, in his life he set us the highest
possible example to follow. But we need more than
instruction just as we need more than a model. We
need help.

It is a plausible saying that "we needs must love the
highest when we see it," but you have only to think of
the earthly life of Jesus to realize that it is far from the
whole truth. Some did love Jesus when they saw him.
Some left everything to follow him and tried to pattern
their lives on his. Others rejected him. Many turned
back from following him and at the end even Jesus'

most faithful disciples abandoned him and he was crucified between two strangers, not with Peter and James and John.

Teaching and example will do little for the worst of men, and even the best of men need more. When we think of Jesus on the cross we see that he is more. He is a Saviour. He is one who comes to release us from the bondage of sin, to open our eyes to the good and empower us to do it. If men were reasonable creatures who knew the difference between good and evil, and always lived up to their own best insights we would not need a saviour. But if we ever were such people, we are so no longer. We are all more or less under the influence of our lusts and fears, and even in our best moments we must say with Paul, "I do not do the good I want, but the evil I do not want is what I do" (Rom. 7: 19). Our human problems are such that we need more than encouragement and advice. We need to be changed.

3. THE PRICE OF DELIVERANCE

It is because of this that the teachers of the church in the early centuries used to speak of the work of Christ as a great rescue operation. Jesus said that the Son of man came to give his life as a ransom for many (Mark 10: 45), and the idea was not hard for theologians to develop. Mankind which really belongs to God has been captured by the devil and is being held up to ransom. God would be within his rights in taking us back by force, but he wishes to act justly, even in dealing with the devil so he ransoms us, redeems us, buys us back (for that is what the word redeem literally means), and the ransom price is the blood of Christ.

Of course this theory raised problems. Should God bargain with the devil? Did Christ escape from the devil on Easter day? In answer it was suggested that God really tricked the devil, using Christ like bait on a fish-hook or in a mousetrap.

It is not hard to see the weaknesses of this idea, but it has a certain vividness and strength and points to two things that need to be emphasized: first, that man's plight is desperate and he cannot save himself; second, that Christ on the cross was not a weak and tragic sufferer but a strong conqueror in whom God was achieving a great victory. This is a proper gospel theme (Col. 1: 13-14; 2: 13-15), and Christian poets have often sounded it.

> The strife is o'er, the battle done;
> Now is the Victor's triumph won;
> Now be the song of praise begun—
>   Hallelujah!

During the Middle Ages, Anselm of Canterbury gave a new twist to Christian thinking about the work of Christ. He objected to the idea that God should be thought of as tricking the devil or as paying him a ransom, and he suggested a new idea. Man, he said, has offended against the honour of God and incurred a penalty far greater than he can pay. If he cannot pay he must go to hell, just as a culprit who cannot pay his fine must go to prison. Christ pays the price of sin for us. He pays the fine, so to speak, and we are released.

John Calvin taught a variant of this theory. According to Calvin, mankind does not have the option of a fine, but is condemned to the sufferings of hell. What Christ did was to bear our punishment for us. In his sufferings on the cross, in his sense of desolation when he cried out, "My God, my God, why hast thou forsaken me?", he was actually bearing in his soul the torments of a person condemned and irretrievably lost, "feeling the severity of the divine vengeance in order to appease the wrath of God, and satisfy his justice."

These theories of Anselm and Calvin have been immensely influential among both Catholics and Protestants and account for the emphasis that has been placed upon the sufferings of Christ in so many hymns and sermons. The theory has the great weakness that it might seem to oppose the love of God to his justice and his holiness, and even to suggest that Christ has to work against his angry and wrathful Father in order to save men. Of course neither Anselm nor Calvin meant to imply that. They knew it was God who in Christ was reconciling the world to himself, but their theory can easily give a wrong impression. Its great strength is that it dramatically sets forth the gravity of sin, the predicament of men and the fact that Christ does for us what we could not do for ourselves.

Obviously none of these theories about the work of Christ is adequate. Yet they do point to something true and valid about God's dealings with us.

4. A SACRIFICE FOR US

This is even more true of the idea of sacrifice, almost a universal idea in the religions of men. Few of us have ever seen an animal sacrificed on an altar or a grain offering made, but almost every primitive people

has sacrifices in its religion. In Old Testament times
many sacrifices were offered in the temple at Jerusalem.
Although Jesus condemned much in the Jewish religion
of his time we have no record that he ever said a word
against the temple sacrifices. He seems to have accepted
sacrifice as a divine institution which taught men something true and important about their relation to God.

What is more he seems to have thought of his own
death as a sacrifice, as though he were offered on the
cross as a sacrificial victim to bear away the sins of his
people. At the Last Supper he said, "This is my blood
of the covenant, which is poured out for many" (Mark
14: 24), and in saying it he was recalling how Moses
had started the Jewish sacrifices at Mount Sinai with
the words, "Behold the blood of the covenant" (Ex.
24: 8).

Many times Jesus seems to have pointed out the connection between his own life and death and the wonderful passages in Isaiah (especially chapter 53) in which
a righteous servant offers his innocent life as a guilt-
offering for his people. It is little wonder that when
the early Christians began to try to explain the cross
of Christ to others they spoke of it as a sacrifice and
believed that that was how Jesus himself had understood it. Peter writes of us as having been redeemed
"with the precious blood of Christ, like that of a lamb
without blemish or spot" (1 Peter 1: 19). The Letter
to the Hebrews goes into the whole matter in the greatest detail showing that Christ is a high priest who offers
himself as a perfect sacrifice. The Revelation speaks of
Christ as a sacrificial Lamb, "standing, as though it had
been slain" (5: 6).

It may be difficult for us who have never seen an animal sacrifice to feel the full force of all this, or to speak as naturally as the early Christians did about having their sins washed away in the blood of Christ. We are more at home among machines than among animals and we associate the word sacrifice most readily with low prices in the stores and high pledges in the church. Though we have a higher standard of living than the people of the Bible it is doubtful if we have any deeper understanding of life. For them sacrifice was a deeply personal thing that could lead them to the very heart of God himself. It should still be so for us.

To think of God as offering his only Son as a sacrifice for our sins is probably still the deepest and most penetrating way of thinking about the atonement. We know, or we can imagine, what it means for a man to lay down his life for his friends. We know or can imagine what it means for the innocent to suffer for the sake of the guilty. We have some experience in our own lives of how suffering accepted freely and borne out of love has the power to redeem. And if we know this we have at least a partial understanding of sacrifice and atonement, and some insight into the mystery of the cross.

5. CHRIST WORKS IN US AS WELL AS FOR US

The second thing that we must say about the work of Christ is that he works in us as well as for us. Our redemption is not something that can take place behind our backs without our knowing about it and without our taking part. We have to participate. It is true that we cannot save ourselves. God must do something for

us that we cannot do, and in Christ he has done it.
Nevertheless, we must respond. God has made us free
and responsible beings and he cannot save us without
a free response. One might almost say that God cannot
save us against our wills, but not quite. That would
be going too far, for it is evident that God does save
people who are stubborn and rebellious and antagonis-
tic by winning their wills and persuades them by the
operation of his graciousness upon them.

Bishop Gore was accused of returning to a superstitious kind of Christianity. He replied by saying:

> Men are indeed prone to superstition; and the
> best definition of superstition is religion which is
> non-moral. . . . Whenever men have proclaimed
> or believed in Christ's atonement . . . as if it could
> be made available for us without our being per-
> sonally changed from evil to good—there is super-
> stition; and the teaching of the prophets and of
> Christ is on no point more emphatic than in con-
> demnation of this sort of superstition.*

The heart of the error against which we have to
guard is the idea that all we have to be saved from is the
penalties of sin, and not sin itself. The wrong way to
think about atonement is to suppose that because we
are sinners we have been condemned to the punishments of hell, but that by some arrangement made
between the Judge and our Advocate, our defence
lawyer, we are to be let off. What we have to be saved
from is not some arbitrary and external punishment
which God has imposed upon us for being sinners, but
sin itself, with its remorse and its bitterness, its fears

The Reconstruction of Belief, John Murray.

and its loneliness, its separation from God which is misery and spiritual death. It is not so much a question of revoking our sentence, it is a question of forgiveness, reconciliation, and restoration into fellowship.

All this does not mean that sin becomes unimportant and forgiveness easy. God is not a vengeful tyrant, but neither is he indulgent and sentimental. It makes the whole matter *more* serious and not less. If it were simply a question of removing the penalties due to sin it might be possible to arrange that by some kind of legal fiction. But if it is a question of bringing us back into God's fellowship that is a much more painful business.

If I quarrel with my neighbour and assault him, a clever lawyer may get me off. But it will take more than a clever lawyer to work on my hatreds and fears and resentments so that I can speak with my neighbour again over the garden fence as a man speaks to his friend. That will be costly for me and for him, and for those who try to bring us back into fellowship. How much more costly and painful to bring a sinner back into the fellowship of the holy God.

Atonement means at-one-ment: making at one. It was to make men at one with God that Christ came to us, suffered for us and works in us.

6. It was God . . .

The third thing we must say about the work of Christ is that it was God himself who was at work. One great drawback to the theories of Anselm and Calvin is that they seem to suggest God does not really want men to be saved. They might even be thought to mean that if

Christ had not interposed himself, God would gladly
have packed them all off to hell. Unhappily they
really have been misunderstood in that way. A little
girl is reported to have said, "I love Jesus, but I hate
God." Of course this was far from what Calvin was
trying to teach and far from the New Testament. But it
shows how things can be misunderstood.

As Donald Baillie wrote, "The crucifixion of Jesus set
men thinking more than anything else that has ever
happened in the life of the human race. And the most
remarkable fact in the whole history of religious thought
is this: that when the early Christians looked back and
pondered on the dreadful thing that had happened, it
made them think of the redeeming love of God. Not
simply of the love of Jesus, but of the love of God."*
Naturally they saw the resurrection as a great demonstration of God's love and God's power. It would not
be surprising if they had thought of the crucifixion as a
temporary defeat of God in which both his power and
his love had been overwhelmed by evil and Christ had
been left as a helpless victim. This is just what they
did not think. From the earliest days the Christians
looked back at the cross as being part of God's purpose
and a revelation of his love.

You can see this in the sermons the apostle Peter
preached in Jerusalem shortly after the ascension, as
reported in the Acts of the Apostles. Naturally enough
he denounces the people for their part in the crucifixion.
It may have been the hands of Roman soldiers, gentiles,
foreigners, lesser breeds outside the law, which actually
drove the nails, but Peter insists that the Jews must

God Was in Christ, Faber & Faber Ltd.

share the responsibility. "It was you," he says, "who crucified and killed Jesus by the hands of lawless men" (Acts 2: 23). It was all a terrible demonstration of human wickedness. *Despite that, it was also part of God's definite plan.*

When you think of it, this was a startling and paradoxical claim. How could so wicked a deed ever be God's will? Is it not almost blasphemy to suggest such a thing? Yet Peter did not hesitate to affirm it time and again in public:

> And now, brethren, I know that you acted in ignorance, as did also your rulers. But what God foretold by the mouth of all the prophets, that his Christ should suffer, he thus fulfilled (Acts 3: 17-18).

No doubt Jesus himself as he journeyed to Jerusalem with his disciples had been preparing their minds for these things, discussing with them the passages in Isaiah 53 about the sufferings of the servant of the Lord, but probably they had not understood. Now looking back they did. Jesus had foreseen this. He knew that his mission was bound to have a tragic ending and that he would be rejected by his own people, but he believed that God could change defeat into victory and turn the wrath of men to his praise. Now they believed it, too, for they had seen it with their own eyes. The cross was not just a manifestation of human wickedness, it was not just a proof of the faithfulness of Jesus, it was a work of the love of God.

Nowhere in the New Testament is there any suggestion of a contrast between the love of Jesus and the wrath of God, nowhere any suggestion that Christ had to suffer to change God's attitude to sinners from one of condemnation to one of forgiveness. If it was Jesus' love for sinners that brought him to the cross, it was also God's love that caused him to give his only begotten Son. In this as in all things Christ and the Father are one. The idea that Jesus died to appease the wrath of an angry God is thoroughly unchristian. It is God himself who pays the price of sin. The great danger of substitutionary doctrines of the atonement is that they obscure this and suggest that only grudgingly and after much coaxing can God be persuaded to forgive. The clear teaching of the apostles is that God himself was at work in Christ bringing the world back into fellowship and reconciliation. There is nothing weak or sentimental about this love. It is a righteous and holy love.

Chapter 11

Salvation

*Not until our self-confidence is shaken
do we feel our need of salvation.
From nature's disasters we are not
spared, but from sin and death and
meaninglessness God will deliver
us if we accept his gift.*

"Are you saved?" How long is it since anyone asked you that question? Or has anyone ever
asked you? It is no longer a very common question and
certainly not always welcome. Anyone who went
around nowadays asking this of every stranger he met
would be thought queer, put down as a fanatic, and
complained about as a pryer into other men's secrets.
Most people who might be asked that question today
would simply not know what to answer. They might
not even know what the question meant. Nor is that
to be wondered at, for in some ways it is a loaded
question, and to know its true meaning you must know

a good deal about the Christian faith.   To give a satisfactory answer you must know even more.

1.   WHAT DOES IT MEAN?

Imagine a Christian in India spying a Hindu holy
man sitting in deep meditation, and asking him, "Are
you saved?"

If the Hindu heard in his trance and deigned to reply,
he might say, "Go away, you foolish man.   I will not be
saved till I have escaped from the body and its lusts,
from the world and the cycle of rebirths, and from
myself, and have become lost in infinite being.   Stop
asking stupid questions, go and work for your own
salvation."

Imagine our questioner asking an earnest young communist, "Are you saved?"   Would he not get some
answer like this?   "Don't ask foolish questions.   Nobody
will be saved till we have established the classless
society, till war and poverty and capitalism have been
abolished.   Then it will be time to ask about salvation.
Stop your reactionary talk and get to work for
socialism."

Or imagine our questioner standing by a stoplight
watching the evening traffic stream out of one of our
great cities.   As the light turns red and a car stops
before him, he asks the young business man behind the
wheel, "Are you saved?"   There is momentary puzzle-
ment, an amused look and then the answer, "I didn't
know I was lost."   Then the light turns green and the
car roars away.

But there are people who would understand the
question.   Ask a young mother after a dangerous and

delicate piece of surgery, or a soldier rescued from an enemy ambush, or a would-be suicide led shivering back from the parapet of a bridge. Are they saved? There can be only one answer. Yes, thank God!

Such people know very well what it is to be saved. Their lives have been in danger. They have stared down into the darkness. And they have been dragged back into safety and light. When they are asked the question, they are not annoyed or disturbed and they have no doubt about the answer. They know that someone else saved them. For them, salvation is both an accomplished fact, a present reality, and they know their saviour.

If Christians persist in asking the question, "Are you saved?", it is because they have been through some experience like this and cannot forget it.

Before the question "Are you saved?" can seem a meaningful question and a reasonable one, you must have been in danger and have been delivered by someone else. If you have lived a life that has always been secure and undisturbed, or if you have always been able to handle the problems that faced you, if things have never got beyond your control, if you can honestly say "I have run my own life," then talk about salvation will never mean much to you.

Perhaps not very many people are so confident in their own powers that they wish to take full credit for running their own lives. We all have been and are dependent on others. Not many of us wish to be so boastful as the Victorian poet who wrote:

> I am the master of my fate
> I am the captain of my soul.

We are less cocksure nowadays, but are we really any less complacent? Modern society has developed such enormous resources that it would be surprising if we did not feel confident in ourselves. Would it be surprising if we were tempted to feel well-adjusted to life and at ease? As individuals we may feel puny and insignificant, but our confidence in human power may be unlimited.

It is not hard to see how idealistic young communists can spurn all belief in God as mere superstition. They have been brought up to believe that science and Marxism can solve all problems. Only as they grow older and experience failure and the limitations of human power will these religious questions come to have meaning for them. For societies as for individuals, *it may take a time of trouble and testing to teach us the wisdom that we ought always to have known: that we are weak, that we are mortal, that we are sinful.* We ought to be aware of these things always, but we hide from them, and it may take illness or failure or humiliation or defeat in war to make men realize the limitations of their power. It may take the shadow of a nuclear war to teach us the fact of our mortality as individuals and as nations. It may take a scandal to remind us of what we always seek to conceal from ourselves: the fact that we are sinners.

Sooner or later those who face the facts of life are bound to see that we do need to be saved and that we cannot save ourselves.

2. SAVED FROM WHAT?

There are three main things from which men seek to be saved: disaster, death, and sin. Much of human

religion is concerned with these things. Primitive tribes-
men dancing rain dances to persuade the clouds to
bring moisture to their crops, or offering sacrifices to
the gods so that their cows will calve or their enemies
will be beaten back in war, may seem a long way from
what we understand as religion. We may dismiss their
beliefs as superstition and magic, but along with the
superstition there must have gone a real sense of man's
insecurity, his dependence on powers outside his
control.

Modern civilization may have done much to tame
nature, but farmers and fishermen know that nature
can still exert her mastery, and storm or drought bring
disaster. Ill health or misfortune can undo the best
efforts. When you have done all that man can do, you
have to say your prayers and trust in God. The prayers
may be craven and unworthy, the trust may be mixed
up with superstition, but running through it all is a
healthy and realistic awareness of man's limitations and
his insecurity. "Fear is better than no God," as George
Macdonald said, and the superstitions of the heathen
may have more real religion in them than the complacency of the comfortable Christian.

It is worth noting at this point that the Christian
gospel does not promise to spare us from the calamities
of nature. As the rain falls on the just and the unjust,
so do the drought and the hurricane. And if some think
they will be protected from harm because they are
devout or because they carry a sacred medal, they did
not learn this from the New Testament.

The second great enemy from which men seek to be
delivered is death. Primitive men or insecure men who
are battling for survival don't have much time to worry

about death; they are too busy trying to live. But when men have built houses for themselves and added field to field and enlarged their barns, they grow to old age and have to face the fact that old age brings weakness and loss of powers and sometimes loneliness. Then it seems that death is the greatest of all the evils from which men need to be delivered, the last conqueror. You may triumph over all your enemies, but death in the end will triumph over you, and his victory is only a matter of time. The world's literature is full of this thought, no doubt because the men who have the leisure to worry about death also have the leisure to write about it.

The Old Testament has little to say about salvation from death, but the New Testament is full of it. As 2 Timothy 1: 10 puts it, "our Saviour Christ Jesus . . . abolished death and brought life and immortality to light through the gospel." It does not mean, of course, that physical death has been removed from the picture. What it does mean is that the gospel has delivered the true believer from being wiped out for ever by death and given assurance that physical death is a door through which he passes into a fuller life. This has made such a difference in the attitude of Christians towards both life and death that it has been said with truth, "The history of Christian dying would be the most thrilling history in literature."

But the third enemy from which men seek deliverance is deeper than either disaster or death. When we see it in ourselves, we call it sin. When we see it in the world about us, we call it injustice. It is moral

evil, and it is concealed behind all other forms of evil.
Moral evil is far worse than natural evil. If a town
is wiped out by an earthquake, we are awed by the
frailty of human life and the irrationality of nature.
But if it is wiped out by bombing, we are filled with
apprehensions of guilt. When a car skids on an icy
road and someone is killed, we tremble to think how
close we often are to death. But when someone is
killed through reckless driving, we face a new and
more dreadful darkness.

3. By whom can we be saved?

If there are three things from which men seek to be
saved, there are also, in the main, three ways by which
they seek their salvation: by relying on their own
actions, by relying on the actions of men in society,
and by relying on the action of God.

Many feel that they can be saved only by their own
efforts to achieve blessedness, by strengthening the
good that is in them and rooting out the evil: Hindus
and humanists are among these.

Others feel that the obstacles in the way of salvation
are too great for anyone to overcome unaided, that what
is required is the work of generations upon generations
of men to establish a perfect society on earth. The
communists believe this, and individual communists
contribute their individual efforts so that some future
generation may reap the benefit.

The teaching of the Bible and the church has always
been that only God can save men, though men themselves both as individuals and as societies are called

to take part in the working out of God's purposes. Why this reliance upon God? Partly because they look for more than a comfortable well-adjusted life on earth, partly because they take more seriously the obstacles to be overcome. It is not just against the ravages of nature that we have to find protection; we have a problem to face in ourselves. It is not only the lusts and appetites of the flesh that we have to subdue; our hearts themselves are deceitful. Advances in science and human understanding will not of themselves establish a utopia, for the infections that corrupt our own lives will taint the societies we build. We are weak and powerless in the face of nature and in the presence of death, but we need more than strength to be saved. We are ignorant of many things, but more knowledge alone will not save us, for we will put our knowledge to bad use.

In the last resort our salvation can only come from God who can save us both from the world and from ourselves and who is not overcome by death as we and our societies are.

It is impressive that in the Bible it is always God who saves. We often tend to think that we must rely on God to forgive our sins or to save us from death, whereas we can save ourselves from lesser evils. But to the men of the Bible *all* salvation comes from God. The prophets of Israel always warned against trusting in political alliances or military weapons.

> Woe to those that go down to Egypt for help and rely on horses, who trust in chariots (Isaiah 31: 1).

> The king is not saved by his great army;
> a warrior is not delivered by his great strength (Psalms 33: 16).

However, when we are thinking of salvation as being delivered not from defeat in battle but from defeat in the battle of life, the surest answer is found only in the New Testament.

The teaching of salvation in the New Testament makes it clear that we are saved through what God has done for us in his Son. Peter makes a startlingly exclusive claim for Christ as the only Saviour in Acts 4: 12. "And there is salvation in no one else," he declares, "for there is no other name under heaven given among men by which we must be saved."

Such an exclusive claim for Christ is an offense to many liberal-minded church people. They would prefer to think that there is good in all religions and all, of whatever faith, who sincerely seek the way of God will be granted the salvation they presumably deserve. This, they would say, is only fair after all.

In reply we have to point out that salvation is not at all something we deserve. It is not at all something we can earn by being good children. It is something to which we have no moral claim, no matter how earnest and sincere we may be. If salvation comes to us, it is God's pure gift.

We have to say furthermore that whether we like it or not God does in fact work through special channels. Though he may send his rain impartially on the just and the unjust, he does not often do this in the Sahara desert. Though many different tribes in the ancient Near East were deeply religious, it was Israel which God chose as the one nation to whom and through whom he would reveal himself. Though there were many devout men in the eighth century before

Christ, it was one man above all else, Isaiah, whom God called to be his spokesman.

This is not something to argue about or complain about. It is a fact of life. This is what happens, and instead of disputing it we would make more sense if we took full advantage of the facts.

In similar fashion God brings his saving purpose for man into focus in one person and one event in time, Jesus Christ and his sacrifice. But through that one person and that one event the blessings of salvation are made freely available to everyone in the world who is willing to fulfil the simple conditions for receiving them.

4. WHAT THEN MUST WE DO?

Perhaps the most difficult question about salvation in this: *how is salvation received* by men; how do they participate in the saving acts of God?

The simplest answer, and the one most widely accepted is just this: you are saved when you die and go to heaven. So far as it goes it is true, salvation is the enjoyment of the fellowship of God in his heavenly presence. But it is not enough to say that. For instance can there be no salvation before death? Can there be no realization of fellowship with God in this life? Is there no sense in which a Christian can say in this life "I am saved"? Of course there is. John speaks of eternal life as something that can and should be enjoyed here and now (John 10: 28; cf. 1 John 5: 11 and 13). To become a Christian, to enter by faith into life in Christ is to know the reality of salvation here and now. So salvation is present as well as future.

Salvation is also corporate as well as individual. We are not saved by climbing our solitary way up into heaven. No man can do that. We are saved by being brought into the fellowship of God in Jesus Christ. There is no such thing as solitary salvation, for salvation implies fellowship. We are brought into the fellowship not only of God but of God's people. This is one of the deeper aspects of church membership, that the one fellowship implies the other. According to the First Letter of John, the one is proof of the other: "we know that we have passed out of death into life, because we love the brethren" (1 John 3: 14), and anyone who does not love his brother can hardly be supposed to have experienced salvation.

This simple fact explains something that worries many people: how can salvation be tied up with an organization like the church? Can't people be saved apart from that? Obviously a mere formal membership in the church is no guarantee that people have appropriated the reality of salvation. But if salvation is a fellowship and a reconciliation, is it not appropriate and even inevitable that it should be passed on and communicated by a reconciled fellowship and received in such a fellowship?

It is one of the marks of a person who has experienced salvation, and knows reconciliation with God, that he cares more and more for others and less and less about himself. One of the very things we need to be saved from is self-centredness and one of the real marks of reconciliation with God is that people cease to think about themselves, even about their own salvation. In a startling verse (Rom. 9: 3) Paul says that he could

even pray to be outcast from Christ if it would do any
good to his kinsfolk, the Jews. It used to be common
to ask candidates for ordination if they were willing
to go to hell for the glory of God: if they would sacrifice
their own salvation for the sake of others. The idea
is of course highly paradoxical. How could a great act
of self-sacrifice break one's fellowship with God? And
how could going to hell glorify God? At least the idea
vividly expresses the fact that salvation can never be a
self-centred thing but leads one into fellowship with
others at the same time that it leads into fellowship
with God.

God's purpose in salvation is not to pluck people up
to heaven by the hair of the head. This false idea has
rightly been caricatured as "extractionist salvation."
The most famous text in the New Testament (John 3:
16) makes clear that the whole world is the object of
God's saving love. That is why it is not enough to think
of salvation as getting up to heaven when you die. The
whole of human history, even the whole of God's creation, has to participate in this salvation. That is why
Paul can speak about the whole created universe waiting with eager longing for the work of salvation to take
its course (Rom. 8: 19) and why the book of Revelation
ends with a vision of a restored and renewed world.
God's purpose is a universal purpose, and though here
and now we can know the reality of his saving love,
we cannot imagine what the full scope of that purpose
will be.

One thing however is clear, that if we know anything
at all about this in our own lives, we cannot want to

keep it for ourselves, or sit back satisfied that we at least are all right with God, whatever may be the case for others. We can only wish to put ourselves at God's disposal, to think no longer about ourselves but only about his will. To have been reconciled to God is to wish to be a reconciler. If the church is a saved fellowship, it must wish to be a saving fellowship.

How it will all work out is a mystery which remains with God. How we can take part in it is a daily discovery and a daily adventure of the Christian life.

Chapter 12

The Life of Grace and Freedom

When we know what God requires of us
are we free and able to do it?
Or do we need help from beyond
ourselves in order to live up to the
commandments of Christ? Real freedom
to do the right is given only by
the grace of God.

In the year A.D. 400 a young British monk, called Morgan, came to Rome. Since Britain in those days was a little known colony out on the edge of the civilized world, while Rome was the centre of politics and business, of culture and religion, Morgan came full of expectancy. What he found filled him with disappointment. Instead of a city of saints he found a city not unlike Montreal or New York today, a city with churches and famous preachers, full of religious interest and religious discussions, but full also of the luxuries and the corruptions of a great metropolis.

We may imagine Morgan, like a secretary from some sleepy Asian country arriving at the United Nations,

147

confused and homesick, pushed around in the street, perhaps being cheated of some of his few pennies. Gradually he becomes more and more convinced of the wickedness of the whole place and works up steam for on outburst of condemnation.

The best seller in Rome at the time was a book of religious memoirs by a North African teacher and churchman. After a lurid youth in which he had committed most of the deadly sins, he was dramatically converted, walked out on his common-law wife and became a monk. The book, as you will readily agree, seemed to have that sure-fire mixture of sex and religion which would excite the interest of any enterprising publisher from that day to this.

It had unquestionable power. But there was something about it which Morgan could not tolerate.

The converted teacher spoke of his sins with great frankness, and he praised God for his conversion as a marvellous work of mercy. How wonderful is God's power! How unspeakable are his mercies! God can do anything: he can even make Christians out of hopeless sinners. God thunders forth his great commands and then by his marvellous grace empowers even the weakest of us to obey them. "Give what thou commandest (O Lord), and command what thou wilt."

1. THE ARGUMENT BEGINS: FREE WILL VERSUS GRACE

Morgan probably felt that it would do these highbrow Romans some good to talk a little less about their religion, and work more at cleaning up their city and their own lives. So he advanced to the attack. It might all have blown itself out with an angry exchange of letters, but as it happened both disputants were men of great ability and the whole Christian world was drawn into a fight, which is still talked about and indeed is still being fought.

The British monk, whom I have called Morgan, is known to history as the arch-heretic Pelagius. The converted professor is known as St. Augustine, and the book is Augustine's *Confessions.*

Pelagius said in effect: God gave us all a mind, a conscience and a free will, and he expects us to use them. Instead of moaning about our sins or praying for God's grace we should be stirring up the powers that we have to lead a better life. We are free to choose between good and bad, and we are responsible for the choices we make. No excuses about the corrupt society we live in, or the bad inheritance we fall heir to, should for a moment obscure the fact of our own responsibility. God will help us, no doubt, if we try to live a good life, but first, last, and all the time, it is up to us.

Augustine in effect replied: No doubt, Mr. Pelagius, you are a well brought up young man and a credit to your school, but you don't know the facts of life. You think it's easy to be good, but you're wrong. It's only easy to be respectable. You think it's easy to overcome temptation, but you don't know much about temptation. If you had ever really had to fight with temptation, had ever really been caught in the grip of passion, you would know that it's not easy to be saved. You would understand why those who have come through say that it was all a miracle, a miracle of the grace of God.

Augustine might have said, though so far as I know he did not, that Pelagius might feel reasonably free of sin because liquor and sex and money were no great problems to him, but there were some other sins he might well look out for: pride, hypocrisy, and pharisaism. And these might be even more dangerous in the end.

The struggle between Pelagius and Augustine was essentially a struggle between the claims of human nature and the claims of God's grace.

The fact that Pelagius has long been regarded officially as a heretic has not prevented decent Christian folk in all ages from thinking that he had a great deal of right on his side. There is nothing surprising about that, for a heretic is not a wicked man, a sworn enemy of the Christian faith who is trying to destroy it. A heretic is a Christian, usually a very intelligent one, who goes off the track while seriously trying to straighten out some point of Christian teaching. The great heretics often come close to the truth. But they are called heretics because in the mind of the church they have not come close enough. I think it is true of nearly all the great heresies over which Christian thinkers have struggled, that they were not false so much as too simple and too one-sided. The truth is more complicated than the heresies.

2. ARE WE ABLE TO DO THE RIGHT?

Now what was the truth Pelagius was fighting for? The first and most obvious was that to talk about the grace of God as Augustine did seemed to destroy human free will and moral responsibility. Surely religion ought to be a summons to action, surely it ought to set men free to serve God freely, surely it ought to send them out into the highways of life able to make up their minds! Augustine with all his talk about grace seemed to be saying that men could do nothing at all by themselves. He seemed to be tying them to God's apron strings, keeping them in perpetual dependence as though God did not want his children to grow up and be free.

You remember the hymn, "Rise up, O men of God!" There is a parody on it which fits the case. Pelagius was complaining that Augustine had re-written the gospel so that instead of being a battlecry it sounded more like this:

> Sit down, O men of God,
> His kingdom He will bring,
> Whenever He desireth it,
> You cannot do a thing.

The difference between these men was no doubt partly a matter of temperament. Augustine was a great, energetic vigorous man: a man of strong temptations and deep repentances. He needed most to be put in harness and tamed for Christ. Pelagius was a steady man, prudent, organized, discreet, the kind who would have made an excellent civil servant. What he needed most was to be pushed out into the world. Both men knew their own needs.

If this were simply a matter of temperament, I dare say most of us would be content to say that we stand on the side of Pelagius and let it go at that. We inhabitants of these cold northern climates are all much alike and we feel very differently from those hot-blooded Italians and North Africans. Most of us probably haven't been drunk more than once or twice in the past year, and haven't had a murder in our families for two generations. But if that were the whole truth, if it were simply a matter of temperament, then the church would have been wrong in calling Augustine a saint and Pelagius a heretic.

I do not think the church was wrong. It seems to me that Augustine, through his deep and vivid experience, learned something that we all need to learn—those of us with the small and whimpering sins as well as the people with the great and crying ones, perhaps more so!

Thomas Carlyle, when he was firmly established as a fashionable author, used to go back to his home in Scotland to visit his old mother. One Sunday after he had gone with her to church and listened to a long evangelical sermon, Carlyle exploded in protest. "If I were a minister," he said, "I would get up in the pulpit and say to the people: Now you all know your duty—go home and do it!" His mother looked at him in silence for a while and then said, "Aye Tammas, and would you tell them how?"

We all complain from time to time about evangelical preaching and often we have something to complain about: few things are more wearing than bad evangelical preaching. But did ever you sit under a man who preached nothing but cold morality? Can you imagine what it would be like to go to church week after week, battered, tired, hopeless, dispirited, and get nothing but stern exhortations to do your duty? "That's all very well," you would say, "but won't you tell us how?"

It's all very well to preach morality, to hold high ideals before people, but there comes a time when men's souls rise up within them and cry: Stop telling us what we ought to do. We know only too well what our duty is. Our consciences are burdened with the knowledge of our duty and our failures to live up to it. What we want is help. It is nothing but cruelty to go on commanding us if you don't show us *how*.

Nobody in his senses would suggest that we do not need to be urged and reminded to do good. Nobody with any experience of life would suppose that that is enough.

Just take a simple Christian duty: You shall love your neighbour as yourself! How can you command anyone to love? How can anyone love from a sense of duty? Aren't the two things incompatible? We know only too well that love can't be commanded. It must be inspired. We go to church and we hear it read from the Bible that we must love our neighbour. We come home determined to love our neighbour. But when we get home our neighbour's car is parked across our driveway. We are about to fire off a salvo when we remember that we must love our neighbour, so we swallow our resentment and let it pass. An hour later we find ourselves thinking that we hate the suits our neighbour wears and we hate the way he blows his nose and we hate—our neighbour. Yet we ought to love our neighbour, so we switch on the TV and think of something else.

Take another simple Christian duty: Do not be
anxious about tomorrow! We know this is true, and we
are glad when the minister reminds us of this duty.
He reminds us that anxious thought is a mark of lack
of faith, that we ought all to examine ourselves and ask
ourselves if we are not failing to trust God in worrying
about the things of the morrow. If all goes well we
will root out this faithlessness, we will stir up the gift
that is in us and give ourselves trustingly into the hands
of God. But supposing we find that our worry has got
the better of us and we read in the Bible, "Be not
anxious." Does that help? No, it makes things worse,
for it drives deeper and deeper into our hearts the
terrible knowledge that we cannot do what we know
we ought to do.

Isn't Christianity a terrible religion, it commands the
impossible! What a cruel, cruel thing to be commanded
to do what we cannot do, being the kind of people we
are. O cruel Pelagius, you who seem so reasonable but
are so unreasonable, you who tell us that we are free
to do good or evil, but do not tell us what to do when
we discover that we are not free!

The trouble with Pelagius (and I think with the
Unitarians, many of whom are modern Pelagians) is
that they begin by making Christianity very simple and
end by making it impossible. When we try the gospel
precepts they turn out to be possible only for people
different from ourselves and better than we are. When
Jesus seems to be telling us to *do* something, he is
really telling us to *be* something, for until we are new
men, we cannot do the things we should.

3. How free are we?

We talk about our human freedom, but how free are we really? We talk of freedom as freedom *from* this or that restriction, but what are we free *for*? We may be free from hunger and tyranny and debt and even from taxes—but are we free to love our neighbour, to be peacemakers?

When I was a student a friend of mine became a communist. He had a real communist conversion. And we used to argue a great deal about freedom. At the climax of the argument he used to say, "What do you mean by freedom? Are you free to jump over the moon?" I never seemed to be free to think of the answer to that one. I suppose the answer is that freedom is far more than the absence of external restrictions, it is the presence of an inner power.

Each time this great argument has been threshed out in history, whether between Augustine and Pelagius or between Luther and Erasmus, one of the key concepts has been *the bondage of the will*. Pelagius in the fifth century and Erasmus in the sixteenth argued firmly for the freedom of the will. Men *can* if they *will*. We don't need more religion, all we need to do is use the religion we have. In other words the followers of Pelagius have always said that we have free minds and ought to use them like free men. To this the reply of Augustine and Luther and their followers, who have generally been regarded as more orthodox, has always been: in theory you may be free, in practice you are not. You may claim that logically you are free to love your neighbour if you will to—but *psychologi-*

cally are you free? You claim to be reasonable men, in full possession of your powers. You claim that your actions are governed by reason and as a rational man you are free. Nevertheless the question remains: "Are you as rational as you think you are? Is a sinner ever really free?"

A famous French film called *La Ronde*, is built on the theme that life is like a merry-go-round, just one thing after another. The story is a sordid one. It is in fact nothing more than a long series of seductions. An Austrian soldier picks up a girl on the street and has a brief affair with her. The girl leaves him for an affair with another man. He leaves her for another girl. And so on for six or seven times till in the end a girl picks up the same soldier with whom the story started. The first two or three episodes make you wonder whether or not you ought to leave. But as the film goes on you begin to see the moral point. Each episode is so intolerably like the last: the same trivial words and gestures, the same deadness and falsity, the same betrayal of personal values.

We often think, don't we, that it's dull to be good. We rather envy those who have the courage to be wicked because their lives must be so much more exciting. But it's not really true! Sin is not exciting! It does not lead to freedom and self-expression, but to imprisonment and bondage.

Virtue is the great adventure! It is fidelity and love and courage and honesty which lead us into the great rewards and fulfilments of life. It is the good man who is really free and the bad man who is repressed and fearful and in bondage. The glorious liberty of the children of God is not just a phrase, but a fact.

The orthodox Christian expression of this point of view about freedom can be seen in the traditional idea of the Four-Fold State:

> *The state of innocence:* Adam in Paradise was free to do either right or wrong. Like an innocent child he was free to act and build up a character.
>
> *The state of sin:* This is the state in which most of us find ourselves when we come to the age of reflexion. We are free in the sense of having a will: but *what* we will is determined by all kinds of fears and prejudices and bad habits. Theoretically we are free, but in practice we are only free to sin, for our wills are in bondage to sin.
>
> *The state of grace:* This is the state in which we are when we have come to know redemption. We have been released from our sins, at least in part. We begin to be free not only to sin, but also to do good. The grace of God has empowered us, has made us willing to do good, has opened up the possibility of good freedom and not just bad freedom. We are still free to do evil, but we are also free to do good.
>
> *The state of glory:* This is the state of the saints and of the blessed in heaven. They are not free to do evil. They simply couldn't do evil. It would be unthinkable for them. They are free only to do good: and that is the highest freedom: the *maxima libertas.*

This is an old-fashioned doctrine. Some day soon I hope we can state it better once we have digested the discoveries of modern psychology, and got them into focus. I feel sure that Augustine and Luther if they were alive today would think that the Lord had sent them Freud and his successors as strange and maybe unwilling allies.

If modern people are doubtful about the bondage of sin, at least they have to admit the bondage of the unconscious self within us. Nobody nowadays is likely to think seriously that salvation is just a matter of obeying the rules: we know now that it is a matter of being remade.

Best of all, no one nowadays has any excuse for thinking that freedom is something we can take for granted. We know it to be something towards which we must constantly strive. Freedom is a great achievement, one of the highest of all. In a very real sense we are only free to be what we are. To enlarge the area of our freedom our character must be enlarged.

The remaking of our character which gives us new freedom is the work of God in us. Only when we quit trying to work it out apart from him can we discover what he is able and willing to do for us. Then we can experience what George Matheson was writing about in his hymn:

> Make me a captive, Lord,
> And then I shall be free. . . .

Chapter 13

The Resurrection and the Life to Come

*If God seeks to save us, we trust it is for
an eternal destiny. Glimpses of this
in the Old Testament become
the strong faith of the New. Christ risen
gives faith that we too shall rise,
whole, new, and not alone.*

Why do we have to talk about life after death at all? Isn't it a very uncertain subject on which there are endless differences of opinion because no one is in a position to speak with authority? Isn't it true that even for those who accept the Bible as authoritative there are still many perplexities and uncertainties here? Why not be content to live this life and let God look after the life to come?

161

1. OUR VIEW OF THE FUTURE AFFECTS THE WAY
   WE LIVE

Why not? Because for one thing the kind of life we
live now partly depends on what we believe about the
life to come, and the convictions we have about this
life imply convictions about the other. Eschatology,
the doctrine about the last things, is not a Christian
eccentricity. Everybody has an eschatology of some
sort. Buddhists believe in Nirvana. Ancient Greeks
believed in Hades. Communists believe in a perfect
classless society which will be ushered in by the last
great revolution. Humanists who place all their trust
in the advance of civilization, hope for a perfect society
on earth. The things we hope for shape our actions,
and without some hope, some picture of what the
future holds, we would not act decisively in the present.

If people believe, as the early communists believed,
that paradise on earth can be ushered in by a workers'
revolution they will go to all lengths to organize it. If
they believe, as several sects do, that the end of the
world is coming within a few years, they are likely
to give up long range social planning and prepare for
the end.

A Hindu, believing that world history will repeat
itself over and over again in endless cycles and that his
salvation lies in escape from the world into eternity,
will see religion as the cultivation of his own soul, but
not as social action.

A missionary in India needed help to carry a sick
man to hospital and appealed to two devout Hindus.
They refused indignantly, saying, "We are holy men,
we never do anything for anyone else."

Even the man who says he has no eschatology, that there is only this life and that death is the end, is no exception to the rule that eschatologies affect your life. His eschatology is a negative one. And the natural conclusion of it can only be, "Let us eat and drink, for tomorrow we die" (1 Cor. 15: 32). There is no escaping eschatology, just as there is no escaping religion, and if you try to do without one, you find that a bad one has forced itself on you.

How, then, are we to decide what is right and what is wrong in this matter? We all want to be scientific when we can, but how can we be scientific here? Psychical research is a long way from telling us what we want to know and we may doubt whether it ever can. For what we need to know is not just what happens to us when we die, but what happens to the human race, to the world and to history. Even if it were possible to prove (as some people claim) that the soul survives death, at least for a time, that would not tell us about the ultimate destiny of the soul or of history as a whole. We cannot observe the last judgment.

If there seems no likelihood that science can help us here, must we draw the conclusion that our beliefs about final destiny and the life beyond death are mere figments of the imagination and always have been? And if so would it not be more honest and more devout to remain firmly agnostic about these things, if that were possible? The answer seems to be that it is not possible to remain neutral and that we will in fact draw conclusions about the other life from what we believe about this one.

Just as the doctrine of creation is not a scientific statement about what happened at the beginning of the world, but an affirmation of God's lordship over nature, so eschatology is not a set of scientific statements about the life after death and the end of time, but an affirmation of God's lordship over life and history. When the biblical writers make statements about death and destiny, and they make them much more cautiously than most people realize, it is not because they thought they had scientific evidence, but because these things must be true if God is what he has shown himself to be.

2. THE BIBLE AND LIFE AFTER DEATH

One of the most impressive things about the biblical teaching on this matter is its restraint. The people of the Old Testament speak very calmly and naturally about dying. We must all die and be like water spilt on the ground (2 Sam. 14: 14). We must go the way of all the earth (1 Kings 2: 2). One day people will look for us and we will not be there (Job 7: 8). They refused to be drawn into a morbid preoccupation with death. What is important is God, and the service of God. For this reason they opposed any attempts to communicate with the dead through spirits and seances (Lev. 19: 31). They thought of these things as a sign of failure to trust in God, and apart from God they were hardly interested in a life beyond. Indeed, the real terror of death was precisely in the fact that one might be separated from God, and the most impressive thing about Old Testament teaching on this subject

is the way in which beliefs about death were transformed by faith in God.

In early times it seems that Israel believed pretty
much what other primitive people believed about the
dead: that they were gathered in Sheol, a dark cave
under the earth (Job 10: 21; Isaiah 14: 9-11). What
seemed to them worst of all about Sheol was not darkness and gloom but being separated from God:

> Sheol cannot thank thee, death cannot praise thee;
> those who go down to the pit cannot hope for thy
> faithfulness (Isaiah 38: 18).

> The dead do not praise the Lord, nor do any that
> go down into silence (Psalms 115: 17; cf. Psalms
> 6: 5).

This may seem surprising, but it should be impressive
to us that the people of the Old Testament were honest
and courageous believers who had the strength to see
that God is far more important than a survival which
is just a gloomy continuation of life on a small pension.
They would have applauded a modern Christian who
said, "Apart from God, I'm not interested in survival."

What matters is God, and it was by thinking about
God that the Hebrews came to have their distinctive
ideas about the life after death. The God in whom they
believed is the same God in whom we believe, but it
takes time to think through the implications of belief in
God and neither they nor we have finished the process.

It took time, for instance, for the Hebrews to see that
God could not be the God of Israel alone, but must be
the God of all peoples. "Are you not like the Ethiopians
to me, O people of Israel?" said Amos (9: 7). This idea

seems to have come like a new revelation, as it still does to some people.

Now, if God is indeed the God of the Ethiopians, and of the whole earth, if he is the Lord of all, must he not rule Sheol as well as the land of the living? Surely even the dead cannot be beyond the power of this rule. You can see this glorious realization that even death cannot come between God and his people breaking like a sunrise in Psalms 73: 23-26:

> Nevertheless I am continually with thee;
>   thou dost hold my right hand.
> Thou dost guide me with thy counsel,
>   and afterward thou wilt receive me to glory.
> Whom have I in heaven but thee?
> And there is nothing upon earth that
>   I desire besides thee.
> My flesh and my heart may fail,
>   but God is the strength of my heart
>   and my portion for ever.

Nothing can separate the believer from God: "If I make my bed in Sheol, thou art there!" (Psalms 139: 8). Not even in death can the guilty man hide from God's judgment: "Though they dig into Sheol, from there shall my hand take them" (Amos 9: 2).

Old Testament thought never got much further than this. The Book of Daniel, the latest book in the Old Testament, takes a further step in declaring that God will raise the dead up out of Sheol at the last day (Daniel 12: 2), and this idea was developed in some detail in Jewish books written in the two centuries before Christ but not included in our Old Testament.

Yet faith in the resurrection of the dead never became a general Jewish belief. The Pharisees believed in it, but the Sadducees did not (Matt. 22: 23 ff.). On this matter, Jesus sided with the Pharisees.

3. THE NEW TESTAMENT FAITH

In the New Testament, faith in the resurrection is no longer debatable. It has become an essential of Christian belief, not so much because of Jesus' teaching but because he himself has been raised from the dead.

Jesus argued (Matt. 22: 32) that if the God of Abraham, Isaac, and Jacob is a God not of the dead but of the living, then Abraham, Isaac, and Jacob must be alive. But Jesus became the supreme instance of his own argument. His followers were quite sure that he had been raised up because it was not possible that he should be held by death (Acts 2: 24). From the very beginning they proclaimed his resurrection as the great visible sign of God's power and of his triumph over death. Death has been swallowed up in victory (1 Cor. 15: 54).

Here the argument is complete. The Old Testament hope that God will raise us up has passed over into the New Testament confidence that he will raise us up as he has raised up Christ. The hope that God would raise men up was always based on a faith in what he is. But now there was a sign, the resurrection of Christ, and the hope it was based on, something he had done. The resurrection is no longer an event in the future; it has become a present fact. Christ is raised up. God has saved us. He has abolished death. He has brought life and immortality to light (2 Tim. 1: 10). The power of the resurrection is already at work in the lives of Christians, so Peter can say that we have been born anew to a living hope by the resurrection of Jesus Christ (1 Peter 1: 3).

The Old Testament glimpsed the resurrection of the dead as an event reserved for the last day by which God would establish his kingdom. In the New Testament the resurrection has already begun. Christ is the first fruits of those who have fallen asleep (1 Cor. 15: 20), and those who believe in him can here and now be like those who have already died (Col. 3: 3) and have been already raised up with Christ (Col. 2: 12 ff; Eph. 2: 1, 5; Rom. 6: 11).

To be sure, the New Testament speaks this way partly by making a play between physical death and spiritual death. The New Testament writers tend to speak of death more gravely than the Old, because they think of death in connection with sin and see physical death as a sign of spiritual death. The sting of death is sin (1 Cor. 15: 56), and to have your sins forgiven by Christ's atoning sacrifice is like sharing in his resurrection. You are raised from spiritual death to spiritual life (Rom. 6: 4). Those who believe in Christ have already passed from spiritual death into spiritual life (John 5: 24).

Physical death still remains but it has now been robbed of its sting. To the Christians death becomes an occasion for the exercise of faith, and an opportunity for love to transform the painful necessity of dying into a willing act of giving up and of self-surrender to God. Many of the evils of the world remain but they have in principle been overcome by God. They have become for the Christian opportunities to witness in action to the love of God. Christ came to establish the kingdom of God, and his resurrection was the sign that he had overcome the powers of evil. But God in his patience allows the old world to continue. He withholds the judgment and the return of Christ to give men time to repent and to believe.

The early Christians believed that the end, and the return of Christ, would be soon. Paul expected to live to see it. They all turned out to be wrong and when they realized it they recalled that it was not for them to know the times or the season (Acts 1: 7). However long or short may be the time between the coming of Christ in humility to announce the kingdom, and his coming in glory to establish it, the resurrection of Christ is for us the sign of God's victory over sin and over death.

4. THE RESURRECTION OF THE DEAD

It may now be easy to see why the Apostles' Creed invites Christians to declare their faith in the resurrection rather than in immortality. The hope that we have for a life after death is not based on confidence in our own inborn capacity to overcome death. Man is a mortal creature for whom death is an enemy that must be overcome. Our mortal nature has to put on immortality (1 Cor. 15: 53). It is by the action of God who raises us up that death can be overcome, not by our own deathlessness.

The Creed speaks, however, not just of resurrection but of the resurrection of the body. This has given rise to some misunderstanding. It does not mean to imply that the actual blood and bones of our present physical bodies will be reconstituted on the last day. Paul wrote that flesh and blood will not inherit the kingdom (1 Cor. 15: 50) and the earlier versions of the Creed which used the word flesh were changed to read *body* to avoid this error. The Creed means that it is the whole man that will be redeemed.

Greek thought in early Christian times held that at death the soul escaped from the body, which was its prison, and went to heaven. This may at first sound a reasonable enough idea to Christians, but on second thought it will be seen to be unacceptable. God is the Creator of all: not just of our souls but of our bodies, and he is concerned not only with our spiritual life, so-called, but with our whole lives: how we eat and drink, how we treat our neighbours, animals, possessions. Nothing in our life is really unspiritual, for God is concerned about it all and has a purpose for it all.

Salvation therefore cannot be thought of as merely the escape of our souls from the body and the material world. It should be thought of as the transformation of our whole life, including our social life, our history, God's whole creation (Rom. 8: 19-22). The phrase resurrection of the body implies that there is no separation of spiritual from material things and no separation of individuals from the society in which they live. Our salvation is a corporate salvation: the word corporate literally means "bodily". There can be no separate salvation for selfish individuals. One of the very things that would prevent our salvation would be selfishness. Only as we give ourselves to God and allow God to work out his saving purposes through us, can we ourselves be saved.

In Paul's writings this is conveyed by the fact that
the word body has a double use. It can mean the
"resurrection body" of the individual, the spiritual body
which the redeemed will have at the end. But body
can also refer to the body of Christ meaning the church,
the redeemed and redeeming community of those who
are saved (or are being saved) by the power of Christ's
resurrection. The individual is not separated from his
environment. Our salvation is a salvation that we
receive "in Christ" as members of the community of
Christ's people.

5. THE FINAL TRIUMPH

The Christian hope is not just a hope for individuals;
it is a hope for the whole human race, even for the
whole world. The sufferings, death, resurrection and
ascension of Christ were not just for his own escape
from a wicked world, nor are they simply the means by
which a few chosen souls may escape. Time and again
the New Testament writers affirm that Christ came to
save not only some but all who will come, not only men,
but the world. The Lamb of God comes to take away
the sin of the world (John 1: 29). God sent his Son
not to condemn the world, but that the world might
be saved (John 3: 17). He is the propitiation for our
sins, and not for ours only but also for the sins of the
whole world (1 John 2: 2). God has consigned all men
to disobedience that he may have mercy upon all
(Rom. 11: 32; cf. 8: 21). As in Adam all die, so also
in Christ shall all be made alive (1 Cor. 15: 22; cf.
Eph. 1: 10; Col. 1: 20). These texts and many others

indicate that the purpose of God's salvation is something far more than the salvation of a few chosen ones out of a hopeless and unredeemable mass. God wills to be all in all, and to reconcile his whole creation to himself.

On the other hand there are texts which clearly teach the exclusion of the wicked from the presence of God. Jesus speaks of everlasting fire prepared for the devil and his angels (Matt. 25: 41), of the worm that dieth not and the fire that shall not be quenched (Mark 9: 48), of the doors of the kingdom locked against those who come too late (Matt. 25: 1-12; Luke 13: 23-27). Paul writes of wrath and fury for the wicked (Rom. 2: 8-11) and John of a sin which is unto death (1 John 5: 16).

These two strains in the gospel have given rise to two contradictory doctrines: first, that the wicked will be punished everlastingly, and second, that the punishment of the wicked will not be endless and that eventually all will be redeemed. For the most part the church has chosen to teach eternal punishment, but the matter was never finally decided. In many parts of the church, especially among the Greek Orthodox, the Anglicans, and liberal Protestants, the matter is left open and it is permitted to hope that all may finally be saved. Eternal punishment has had strong defenders in men like Augustine, Thomas Aquinas, and John Calvin, but by teaching it so as to make God seem harsh and unrelenting they have always led to a reaction against the doctrine.

The truth seems to be that the testimony of scripture is not sufficient to establish either doctrine against the

other. There is clear teaching in scripture that the
wicked will be punished and God's justice established,
but whether the punishment will be hopeless and endless is less clear. The only texts which seem explicit are
Matthew 25: 41 and Revelation 20: 10. On the other
hand there is the strong and clear teaching that God's
purpose will triumph, and that his purpose is to reconcile the world unto himself. But will God save men
against their will? Does the "dread gift of freedom"
which God has given man not carry with it the freedom
to reject God and one's own blessedness? The answer
seems to be yes. And if it is, then no one can claim
that all men *must* be saved. At the most, we may hope
that they may.

Perhaps wisdom lies in recognizing the truth on both
sides, both the greatness of God's love and the terrible
consequences of sin, and remembering that it is God
who holds the issues in his own hand. We do not need
to know the answers to these ultimate questions, and
God has told us enough for our obedience here and
now. We dare not lull men to sleep with the kindly
assurance that all must be saved in the end. The
dangers of sin are real and urgent. On the other hand
we must not say anything to suggest that the grace of
God in Jesus Christ is not strong enough to deal with
the wickedness of men. Our duty is to see and proclaim
and live by the lovingkindness of God in Jesus Christ,
and to believe in its power to redeem.

PART THREE

The Church and the World

Chapter 14

The Holy Spirit and the Christian Life

The vigour of the early church
came from the presence of the Holy
Spirit. He speaks through scripture and
makes it living for us. He is Lord
also of the church, and the power of God
in the life of Christians.

In the early years of the church the questions must often have been asked: what can ever make up for the loss of Jesus' earthly presence among us? Can those who have not known him in the flesh ever overcome this handicap? When the apostles, who did know him, die out, will it ever be the same again, or must the church not dwindle and lose its power as his memory fades?

These questions are quite understandable. You can read them between the lines of many New Testament

177

passages (for example, John 14-16). Whatever the
answer was, the church certainly did not dwindle and
die but grew in strength and vigour generation by
generation.

1. THE EARLY CHURCH WAS VERY MUCH ALIVE

There is something profoundly impressive about the
early church. By all human reckoning, it ought to
have been a failure. The disciples of Jesus seem to have
been very ordinary men, and right up to the crucifixion
seem to have had a very imperfect understanding of
Jesus' purpose. At the crucifixion they deserted him.
At the end Jesus was alone on the cross and the disciples were scattered in fear and remorse and confusion.
Any impartial observer would have said that finished
that. Far from being the end, it was the beginning.
What made the difference?

First, the resurrection, which turned defeat into
victory. On the morning of Easter day, the disciples
were confused and disappointed. On the evening of
Easter day, these same men were transformed into
convinced believers, moved to the depth of their being
by what God had done, and filled with a quiet steady
certainty which was to outlast the years and carry them
to the ends of the earth. They were witnesses of the
resurrection and so much did it mean to be a witness
of the resurrection that even Paul who was not one of
the disciples, staked his claim to be an apostle on the
fact that he too had seen the risen Christ on the road
to Damascus.

But who could take the place of the apostles, and
what could take the place of the knowledge of Christ
in the flesh, or the sight of him in his risen glory?

The question is not easily answered, but it has to be faced. The facts of history compel us to face it; the fact that the church did not die out after the first generation. There is no indication that it even faltered in its conviction as the leadership of the church passed from those who had known the Lord in the flesh and in the resurrection to those who had not. The New Testament gives a straight answer to this question. It was the coming of the Holy Spirit that made up for the loss of the earthly Jesus.

According to John's Gospel, Jesus promised that a Counsellor, the Holy Spirit, would come to take his place (John 14: 16, 26), and it was even to the church's advantage that he should go away, for until he left, the Spirit could not come (John 16: 7). There are two accounts of how the Spirit did come. According to the fourth Gospel, it was before the ascension (John 20: 22); according to Acts it was on the day of Pentecost (Acts 2: 1 ff.). In either case the gift of the Spirit followed the completion of Jesus' ministry on earth.

2. THE SPIRIT SPEAKS IN THE BIBLE

If you ask the average Protestant what was left to Christians once Jesus had gone, he will probably reply not that it was the Spirit, but that it was the Bible. Jesus' teaching about God, man and human life was gathered together by his followers. In front of it was placed the Old Testament which is the necessary background for understanding Jesus. Behind it was placed the story of the beginnings of the church, and the Bible was complete. The memory of the earthly life of Jesus might now fade from the minds of men, but though this was no doubt a heavy loss, there was compensation in the fact that his teaching and the whole counsel of God were now safely preserved in writing and available to every man, woman and child for ever.

Such an idea may seem less exciting to us than it did to early Protestants, for we probably have less enthusiasm for book learning and less confidence in its power to save than they had. To them it was thrilling. In their day printing was still a novelty and books a rarity. The thought that an ordinary man might possess and read a Bible of his own, in his own language, was immensely exciting. To the early Protestant, the Bible, available in his own hands, was the most revolutionary thing imaginable. Until the invention of printing, very few people could expect to own a Bible, and there was little to encourage the average man to learn to read. The Bible, moreover, was kept in a strange language known only to the learned and was guarded closely by the clergy. No wonder the Bible in print seemed to bring religion within reach and to make Christ real as he had not been since the days of his earthly ministry.

It is hard for us to imagine how exciting Bible reading was to these early Protestants. The best parallel we can think of is that of a South American Roman Catholic peasant converted to Protestantism and taught to read. Things that had been reserved for learned discussion among the experts were suddenly opened up for all Christians. Everyone was being urged to share in the task of discovering God's will. No wonder they felt that the church, which had been asleep for centuries, had come awake, and the Lord, so long absent

from his church, was again teaching his people through
his book.

Why does Bible reading not give us the same sense
of excitement and discovery? For several reasons.
Books as such have lost their scarcity value. We read
more than people have ever read. We have more books
and magazines available than we have time to look at.
The Bible was once the only book people had. Now
it is one among many, and less easy to read than most.

Then, the Bible has lost its publicity value. When a
book is forbidden by the censor, everyone wants to
read it. When the Bible was a forbidden book to the
common man, reading it was an adventure. It still is in
communist countries where Bibles are scarce. But
when a Bible is to be found in every hotel bedroom,
it tends to be treated as part of the furniture.

A third reason is that Bible reading too easily
degenerates into memory work. It is one thing to
memorize the ten commandments, the beatitudes,
and Paul's great poem of love, 1 Corinthians 13. It is
quite another to hear the word of God and meet Jesus
Christ in the reading of scripture. The great reformers
were well aware of this and constantly warn that Bible
reading may lead to nothing but book learning unless
the Holy Spirit speaks through the words of scripture,
breathing life into them and making them for the reader
a living word of God.

Without the Spirit, the Bible remains dead history,
and the church which reads it can only look back wist-
fully to the days when Jesus was here among men. With
the Spirit, the Bible becomes living history, still being

written in our own lives, and Jesus becomes a leader at work among us.

The Bible cannot really be said to "take the place of Christ" in the life of the church. Some phrases in the opening pages of *The Westminster Confession of Faith* might seem to suggest that, for instance, when it says that God's former ways of revealing himself to his people are now ceased and that what God wishes to say to his people he has now committed wholly unto writing. However, *the Bible is not a substitute for a dead and absent Christ; it is a witness to the living power of Christ.* When Christ spoke to his disciples about his departure, he did not say that the Bible would take his place, but that the Spirit would.

One way in which the Spirit does this is to speak to men through the Bible, leading men to understand it, to recognize Jesus Christ, about whom they read in the Bible, for what he is, and so draw them into fellowship with him. In his days on earth, Jesus called other men "to be with him." In the reading of scripture, the Spirit calls men to fellowship with him in the life of the church.

3. THE HOLY SPIRIT IN THE LIFE OF THE CHURCH

To the question, "What was left to Christians when the earthly life of Jesus was over?" the average Protestant might reply, "The Bible," but the average Catholic would reply, "The Church." Neither answer is complete. The Bible does not exist apart from the church, and the church does not exist apart from the Bible, and both Bible and church depend for their power on the activity of the Holy Spirit. Let us look at both the truth and the falsity in the average Catholic's answer.

It is obviously true that Jesus did leave a church behind him. His disciples were left behind to carry on his work. That is indeed more obvious than that he left the Bible behind. For the books of the New Testament were written within the church. But in what way did Jesus leave the church behind him?

Roman Catholics are accustomed to lay great stress on one text in the Gospels, Matthew 16: 18, where Christ says, "You are Peter, and on this rock I will build my church." They claim that Jesus handed on his authority to Peter, who became the first bishop of Rome, and that all authority and all power in the church comes from Christ to Peter, from Peter to his successors, the popes. From popes it is parcelled out to bishops, then to priests, and so down to ordinary church members and the world at large. So deeply do Roman Catholics feel about this that Pope Pius XII could write, "The Church is, as it were, another Christ."

Protestants must be careful not to react so violently against these ideas that they deny the elements of truth in them or belittle the place which the church should have in the purposes of God. It is possible, even probable, that Peter became head of the Christian community at Rome. It is certain that the church of Rome gained great authority among Christians in the early centuries. There can be no doubt that church government by bishops is very ancient and honourable. Whatever its faults, the church of Rome has great achievements to its credit and we ought to admire them. We do not wish to follow it in all its ways. Still, we cannot be content to be negative, but must seek a truer doctrine of the church and a fuller concept of ministry.

It will help us to a truer understanding if we remember that the church should never be separated from the Bible or from the Holy Spirit. The fundamental Protestant objection to the Roman position is that it makes the church mistress over the Bible and controller of the Spirit.

It may be true historically that the Bible was written in the church and that the church had to decide what books should or should not be included in the Bible. But in doing this, the church was not demonstrating its authority over the Bible. It was saying to itself and to the world:

> This is the message we have received. We did not make it up and we cannot change it. We are only allowed to transmit it and to publish it. We may try to explain it, or defend it, or work out what is implied in it, but in setting this book apart from all other books we acknowledge its authority over us. And we warn everyone that what the church says is only commentary on what the Bible says and is to be judged by its faithfulness to the Bible.

Where a church puts its own teaching on a level with the Bible or fails to recognize that the Bible stands in judgment over what it says, it goes wrong.

It is obvious that on many issues the Bible does not give explicit guidance. The churches and individual Christians will often have to make up their own minds without much direct help from the scriptures. But what they say or do ought always to express the spirit of the biblical message. Always they ought to be trying to keep their thought and action in line with the gospel.

The church is no more controller of the Spirit than it is mistress of the scriptures. When the disciples journeyed with Jesus they shared in his work, but always acted under his authority and were subject to his correction. Before his departure, he promised that he would send the Holy Spirit to take his place. When Jesus says that the Spirit will take his place, he means that the Spirit will be the church's Lord just as he was the disciples' Lord, or rather that he will exercise his lordship over the church "in the Spirit" just as he exercised his lordship over the disciples "in the flesh." The New Testament frequently speaks about the Spirit as "the Lord" (2 Cor. 3: 17), just as it speaks of Jesus as the Lord, and Paul does not make a clear distinction between being "in Christ" and being "in the Spirit."

This means it is a mistake to think that the apostles or Peter took over the authority of Christ and, instead of being servants, became lords themselves. "What we preach is not ourselves," said Paul, "but Jesus Christ as Lord, with ourselves as your servants for Jesus' sake" (2 Cor. 4: 5).

The church must continue to be a servant church, as much under the authority of the Spirit today as the disciples were under the authority of Jesus in the days of his flesh. It is quite wrong to think of the church or any minister of the church as being the vicar of Christ as if it or he were endowed with the authority of Christ. That authority rests in the Holy Spirit and the church can transmit or exercise it only "in the Spirit." The church is not put in control of the Spirit, to use the power of the Spirit as and where it wills. *The church is put under the power of the Spirit to do the will of the Spirit, which is the will of Christ.* The church does not inherit the authority of a dead and departed Christ and use the power of the Spirit to exercise that authority. Christ lives and reigns in his church through the power of the Spirit.

4. THE LORD IS THE SPIRIT

We began by asking the question which the disciples and the early Christians must have asked: "What can compensate us for the loss of the earthly, physical presence of Jesus here on earth?" We saw Jesus' answer, that the Spirit would take his place, and that his authority would now be exercised by the Spirit which is Lord as he was Lord. This is not a different authority, however, because the Spirit is the Spirit of Christ and the Spirit of God. The authority of God, of Christ, and of the Spirit may be distinguished, but they are not different, and this is what the doctrine of the Trinity means when it affirms the unity of the three persons in the Godhead.

Neither the Bible nor the church is a person of the Trinity. Their authority is always the authority of the Spirit who speaks through them and lives in them. The Bible is the word of God only as the Spirit testifies in and through it. The church is a divine society only as the Spirit dwells in it and works through it. To claim divine authority for the Bible as a human book or the church as a human institution is idolatry, and God will disown it.

Idolatry seems to be a permanent human temptation, though we see it more clearly in others than in our-

selves. Protestants are quick to denounce idolatry in
the Roman church and to claim that the pope puts
himself in the place of God when he claims infallibility
for his *ex cathedra* utterances. They suspect the Roman
church of wanting to possess and manipulate divine
power by channelling it through the clergy and the
sacraments.

Are Protestants not open to the same temptation
when they try to use the Bible as an instrument
of spiritual dictatorship, as some do, claiming for themselves the authority of God because they have in their
possession an infallible book? Protestants are sometimes annoyed when the pope claims to speak for
Christ. Are they any better when they try to defend
their own opinions from criticism with the phrase "The
Bible says . . ."?

God will and does act through the church. He will
and does speak through the Bible, but only by the
power of the Spirit. And one condition of the Spirit's
working is that we should acknowledge him as our
Lord. The Spirit is God and God will not allow himself
to be *used* by men even for the highest purposes. But
he is always ready to use men who put themselves at
his disposal. The Spirit will empower the church if it
puts itself in the role of a servant. The Spirit will speak
through the Bible to those who humbly seek guidance
there as to God's will for them and the tasks he wishes
them to do. But whenever we try to make God speak
through the Bible to confirm our own opinions, or try
to use the church for our own earthly purposes, God
will disown us. He will not be mocked and he will not
be used. He is the Lord.

The difference between magic and religion, it is often

said, is that in magic men try to use divine power to get what they want, whereas in religion men seek to praise God, worship him, and serve him. If this is true, then we must always be on our guard lest we turn religion into magic. Read the story of Simon the magician in Acts 8, and ask whether the temptation he faced is not more common than we like to admit.

5. The Spirit in the Christian's life

The Holy Spirit is God, present and active in the Christian fellowship and in the life of the Christian. In Acts 2 we find the story of the experience at Pentecost when the Christians gathered together in one place became filled with the Holy Spirit. This incident was one of those rare, exalted and deeply moving occurrences that may happen once in a lifetime, but leave everything changed.

It was an exciting and emotional experience. Those who would love to recover the first fine rapture of apostolic Christianity sometimes jump to the conclusion that the emotional experience is the main thing to reach after. Others, who are suspicious of emotionalism, or afraid of their own feelings, prefer to ignore this side of the story as much as possible. It is a mistake to think that the excitement of this moment is the main thing. Religious excitement should not be sought after for its own sake; neither should one shrink from it. The main thing is to be so open to the inflow of the Spirit of God that in his own time and in his own way he may come upon us with power. When that happens, what is more natural than that our feelings should be deeply stirred?

It was a congregational experience that happened at

Pentecost. It was to the Christian fellowship that the Spirit came rather than to individuals in solitary meditation. Sharing together in this experience must certainly have made the fellowship much deeper than it had been before, for the reality of God's presence was a shared and unforgettable experience. It suggests to us that one thing we ought to strive for in the church is that kind of fellowship of faith and openness into which the Holy Spirit can come.

This was also an experience that changed people. It was at this point that the Christians turned from waiting to witnessing. Hitherto they had been meeting and praying together more or less in private, waiting for something to happen that would show them what to do next. When the Holy Spirit came there was a fulness and an overflow of joy and confidence. The Spirit gave them utterance, and from that time they began to speak out publicly, witnessing to the gospel of the risen Christ, and winning others to faith in him. This also the Holy Spirit can be expected to do for us.

It was an experience with lasting results. The excitement of Pentecost died down, naturally enough. But the Holy Spirit had demonstrated his power and presence among the members of the church, and this they never forgot. They sought his continued presence to guide and lift their life, and the New Testament bears witness that they did not seek in vain. Whether or not we pass through an experience such as that at Pentecost, it is the Holy Spirit on whom we depend to draw us into closer fellowship with God, to give us the power of an overflowing life, and to make our fellowship in the church what it ought to be.

Chapter 15

The Church

> *Though imperfect the church is*
> *necessary, and to be a Christian one*
> *must be a member of the church.*
> *What is the nature of the church? And*
> *what are the ministries to which*
> *we are called?*

"Christianity has no meaning for me whatsoever apart from the church," says J. H. Oldham, "but I sometimes feel as though the church as it actually exists is the source of all my doubts and difficulties."*

You can see what he meant. There are plenty of ugly things about the church. It has a marvellous history of heroism and service and compassion. It also has a shameful record of bigotry, persecution, and selfishness. Judged as a human institution it has enormous achievements to its credit, but also some depressing crimes. And if you take a sharp look at the people who go to church you will find that they include some of the

---

*J. H. Oldham: *Life Is Commitment*, SCM Press Ltd.

finest of men, but also some who are selfish and far
from a credit to the Christian faith. And yet you can't
imagine Christianity without the church. Why?

1. WHY THE CHURCH IS NECESSARY

Why is it that when people say: "I don't go to
church, but I'm a better Christian than most of those
who do," we feel compelled to say to them, "Then you
don't understand the church, and you don't understand
Christianity either." Even if there are people outside
the church who are nobler, more generous, more self-
sacrificing than many inside, that does not change the
fact that *to be a real Christian you must be a member
of the church.* There may be civilians braver and more
resourceful and more patriotic than anybody in the
army, but that doesn't change the fact that to be a
real soldier you must be enlisted.

Of course, when we talk about the church in this
way we are talking about something more than a building full of pews and stained glass windows, more than
the congregation of Christians who meet there for
worship, more than a denomination such as the United
Church or the Lutheran or the Baptist. We mean something very exalted indeed: the whole company of God's
folk whom he has gathered, in all ages out of all
peoples, to be his people and live in fellowship with
him not only in this life but always.

When the New Testament talks about the church
it uses the Greek word *ecclesia* from which we get
ecclesiastic and ecclesiastical. The literal meaning of
that word is "called out." God is calling people to come
out and serve him, and live with him. The church con-

sists of those who have come out in answer to the call. It is almost as though the Lord had said that he doesn't want any conscripts in his army, only volunteers. Queer people may volunteer, and many who would make good soldiers may stay home, but that is how he wants it. He takes only those who are willing to come.

Many in the church may not look very fit for active service. They have grown weary in well-doing. For them Christianity has become merely a habit. They groan and grumble about the conditions of service. There are people like that in every army. But a great general can do wonders with them, filling them with new hope and vitality so that the ordinary Joe turns out to be a hero. We ought to look for that in the church too, and if we look for it we will surely find it.

But even when you have made all the excuses and allowances somebody may well say to you, "Isn't there still something unfair about the very idea of a church? Why should some people have an advantage while others are left outside? Surely it is unworthy to suggest that God is so unequal in his dealings."

This is a very real difficulty and it probably bothers people who could not put it into words. How unfair of God to work through the church! Why can't any one come to God without having to associate himself with an organization like the church?

If the trouble with us was just ignorance or laziness, and if we could put these things right by working harder at being religious, then perhaps we would have no need for a church. There are religions like that. They teach that a man or woman can go it alone, developing his own spirituality. He may benefit by the

example of others, he may be helped by the instruction
and inspiration of religious experts, he may be encouraged by the fellowship of a religious society. These
things may be helps, but they are not strictly necessary,
and if you can do without them and go it alone so much
the better for you.

Christianity is not that kind of religion. It teaches
that what is wrong with men is that they are at war
with themselves and their neighbours because they
have fallen out of fellowship with God. The cure for
our ills, and the very essence of salvation is the restoration of harmony between God and men. Reconciliation
is both the means and the end of Christian salvation,
and the Christian community is the place where we
learn to live in fellowship and get our first taste of what
the life of the redeemed is like. The church is a
voluntary society, in the sense that people have to be
persuaded to join it. You defeat its purpose if you
try to coerce people into its ranks. But *if you want to
be a Christian, church membership is not optional.*
There may be such a thing as solitary religion, but
there is no such thing as solitary Christianity. The
Christian life is a life of fellowship with God and man
and a life of service to God and man.

The same point can be made in another way. How
can you communicate the Christian faith, and show
people what Christianity is all about? In books? In
lectures? These may help, but in the end it must be
done through people's lives, through actions, and
through a community. God himself, if we may dare
to speak this way, could take no other course. He
had to send his Son to be a "man for God" and a "man

for other men," to draw people into fellowship and to create a community. The gospel of reconciliation can only be shown forth by a reconciled and reconciling fellowship.

2. THE NATURE OF THE CHURCH

The Nicene Creed describes the church as being *One, Holy, Catholic,* and *Apostolic* and these four adjectives have become traditional ways of pointing to the nature of the church.

(*a*) *One.* In what sense is the church one? Obviously there have to be local congregations in different places. There always have been. Obviously as the church grows and spreads there will come to be groups of churches speaking different languages: Greek, Latin, French, English, Chinese. If by the accidents of history these churches come to be separated from one another by long periods of time they come to develop ways of life which are quite different from one another. In some places church services will be plain and austere, in others full of elaborate ceremony and colour and music. Different systems for church government and administration will grow up at different times and places.

None of these things are bad. Indeed variety in customs and habits will be wholesome and even necessary. But when Christians cannot agree about essentials something has gone wrong. When differences between Christians give rise to hatred and suspicion and violence then the gospel itself is being denied. Who will believe that we have a gospel of reconciliation if we cannot be reconciled among ourselves? How can we expect people to believe that Christ has broken down the dividing walls of hostility and made us all one, if Christians cannot themselves be one in Christ?

The ecumenical movement, which has been called the great new fact of our time, is not an attempt to build a super-church, a religious power bloc. It is an attempt to reconcile divided Christians to one another so that they and the world may be reconciled to God. A church divided against itself contradicts its own nature just as scandalously as a temperance society whose members are always getting drunk. We don't need and maybe should not want a super-church administered from one centre. Nor should we look for uniformity in worship or in procedure. But we should strive to be agreed on essentials. We should treat one another as those who have been reconciled in Christ. We should be one as God is one.

(*b*) *Holy.* In what sense is the church holy? Is it because its members have achieved a high level of moral and spiritual character? Not really. Though personal righteousness is one of the aims and marks of the Christian, we too often fall short of the standards we should attain. In the last resort it is God alone who is holy, and Jesus Christ is the holy One of God because through him God accomplishes his work. In the Old Testament the sabbath, the law, the temple, the people of Israel itself, are holy because these are the things which God has appointed and through which he works. In this sense a thing is holy because it has been set apart and consecrated for the service of God.

So the new Israel, the Christian church is holy because it has been chosen and consecrated for God's work (1 Peter 2: 9). But those who are called to the service of the holy One must strive to be holy themselves. "You shall be holy, for I am holy" (1 Peter 1: 16). The people are called to offer their bodies as a living sacrifice acceptable to God (Rom. 12: 1), and to sanctify themselves (Eph. 1: 4; 5: 26). But holiness is not our own achievement; it is something that is worked in us through membership in the holy community and which the community derives from its fellowship with God. When the church or individual Christians fail to show the marks or the fruits of holiness we are denying our true nature.

(c) *Catholic.* It is one of the curiosities of church history that the word catholic should have come to be a party name. One group of Christians calls itself the Roman Catholic Church. One party in the Anglican communion is called Anglo-Catholic. Many among ourselves feel that if you are a Protestant you are therefore not catholic. All this shows confusion and misunderstanding. The word catholic means general or universal. So its primary use is to refer to the world-wide universal church as distinguished from local Christian communities.

Its secondary use is to designate the orthodox church, the church with the true doctrine and in the true tradition. Now if the Roman church believes that only those in communion with the bishop of Rome are members of the true church and all others are heretics and schismatics then they are of course justified (according

to their own lights) in denying the right of anyone else
to be called catholic. And if you believe that they
are right the only reasonable thing to do is to join
them.

But if you are a Protestant (or Anglican or Orthodox
for that matter) and believe that your denomination
is truly Christian, has not denied the true faith or for-
feited the true fellowship, then you must claim to be
part of the one universal church and that means claiming to be catholic. It would be foolish and inconsistent
to do anything else. And it would be a betrayal of our
reforming forefathers not to do so. They reformed the
church in order to be more faithful to its true nature,
and in order to be more catholic and not less. They
believed that it was the Roman church which had
departed from the original catholic faith by its innova-
tions, and they sought to return to the pure doctrine
of the early centuries. The Swiss Reformed Church in
its *Confession* of 1566 wrote:

> Since then we are every one of us of this faith and
> religion, we trust that we shall be held by all not
> for heretics but for Catholics and Christians.

(*d*) *Apostolic.* The word apostle means "one who is
sent," and is used to describe the chief disciples of
Christ who were sent out by him after his resurrection
and before his ascension to make disciples of all nations.
To say that the church is apostolic is therefore to claim
that it is the church which resulted from the missionary
work of the apostles and therefore from the work of
Christ. Paul wrote to the Ephesians that as members
of the household of God, they were built upon the

foundation of the apostles, Jesus Christ being the chief cornerstone (Eph. 2: 20).

The term also means that just as the disciples were sent out so the church is sent out into the world to continue the same work. An apostolic church is a missionary church "sent out" to make disciples of all nations. A church which fails to be missionary, forgets about others, and is content to look after itself, forfeits the claim to be apostolic and denies its nature as a church.

It is not for us to set down the conditions of church life: our Lord has given them to us. We are to go out and preach the gospel. Neither is it for us to devise new gospels. The only authority we have is what we get from Christ, and it is an authority to be his ambassadors and representatives and to deliver his message. It is not our business to invent new messages of our own; if we do so it will be on our own authority and not on Christ's.

We will need every ounce of imagination and strength we have to interpret his purpose and commend his message in our own day. But while we may not alter or change the gospel we have to proclaim, we do not need to apologize for it or feel anxious for its success. If the church and the gospel are truly apostolic God will bless them in his own way and in his own time.

3. MINISTRY IN THE CHURCH

The word minister is Latin for a servant, and so ministry means service. We tend to think of the

ministry of the church as the work of preachers and
pastors. The idea is far wider than that.

The first and basic ministry in the church is the
ministry of Christ. It was he who said, "Whoever
would be first among you must be your slave; even as
the Son of man came not to be served but to serve";
not to be ministered unto, but to minister (Matt. 20:
27ff.). He was a true and perfect servant of God being
completely faithful to the end, and he called his church
to follow him in this service. The church as a whole is
called to minister, to be a servant of God and to serve
others in the name of God. It is quite a false idea to
suppose that the church is composed of two classes,
the ministers and the laymen. *Every Christian has
some ministry or service* to render in the church, while
the word "lay" comes from the Greek *laos* which means
the whole people of God which is the church. In this
original sense every layman has a ministry and every
minister is a member of the laos.

One of the important developments in the church
today is the recovery, almost the rediscovery, of the
ministry of the laity. Lay men and women are re-
discovering that their service and witness are essential
to the life of the church, and indeed to their own
growth as Christians. It is a mistake to depend on the
ordained ministers to shoulder the load of responsibility
for spiritual leadership. Every church member has a
ministry, and he performs this in his home, and where
he works, and among his friends as well as within the
meetings of the church.

Mohammedanism is spreading rapidly in Africa
south of the Sahara in our time. We are told that one

of the chief reasons is that every Muslim is a missionary for his faith. His is a layman's religion. This is a challenge and a rebuke to us Christians who, when we go about our business at home or abroad, give so little sign of the faith that is in us.

But not all the members have the same function, as Paul says (Rom. 12: 4). The hand, the foot, and the eye have special functions in the body, each with its own place and its own dignity and so in the church there are different kinds of ministry of which Paul enumerates among others: apostles, teachers, helpers, and administrators (1 Cor. 12: 14-31).

Exactly what these different ministries were it is hard to say. There has been a great deal of controversy in recent times about the different grades and types of ministry. In nearly all churches some people are ordained and set apart to special service which includes preaching, pastoral care, teaching, and the administration of the sacraments, and it is common, though not quite accurate, to refer to them as "the ministry." Some Anglicans claim that there are three orders or grades in this ministry: bishop, priest, and deacon. Among Presbyterians, Methodists, and Congregationalists, and therefore in The United Church of Canada there is only one order. All ministers are equal though some may be appointed to special offices such as the moderatorship. Episcopal Methodists and many Anglicans would claim that bishops have the same order as other ministers, and only a special office. Some agreement on these matters will have to be found if there is to be union between episcopal and non-episcopal churches.

The question is sometimes asked whether the ministry comes from above or from below, that is, whether ministers are appointed from above by bishops or from below by the congregations which they are to serve. Roman Catholics are supposed to represent one extreme and Congregationalists the other, while most churches have a compromise system where ministers are appointed by the bishop or by the presbytery (which exercises the functions of a bishop) with the consent and agreement of the congregation. In a more profound sense the ministry certainly comes from above, from God. It was Christ who appointed a ministry in the church, not men who decided that it might be useful.

And it is Christ who calls men and women to that ministry. No one can decide to become a minister and take the ministry upon himself. There must be an inward call, and before the church will give an outward call by ordaining anyone to the ministry it must satisfy itself of the reality of the inward call.

What we have been saying can be gathered up best in the idea of the church as the body of Christ (Eph. 4: 16). If you are Christ's man or Christ's woman you are part of this living body, the church, whose head is Christ. By this body you are nourished and sustained. And you have your proper ministry to perform, a special function to which you are called, whether as a lay or as an ordained member.

The means by which we are nourished in this body of Christ, and the work which this body is called to perform in the world are dealt with in the next chapters.

Chapter 16

The Means of Grace

*The Spirit of God reaches and influences
believers through special channels.
Chief among these are the Bible,
baptism, the Lord's Supper, prayer,
and common worship.*

In so many ways God can make himself
known to us. When a golden sunrise or a crocus breaking open in the spring stirs us to think of God, this is a
way in which he makes himself known to us. So he may
break through into our hearts while we listen to music
or gaze on a picture or meet with old friends.

Anything which may be used by God's Spirit for
reaching and influencing men could be called a means
of grace, a channel for his love.

In the Christian's experience, however, some channels
are much better than others. In the words of Isaac
Watts,

The heavens declare Thy glory, Lord,
In every star Thy wisdom shines;
But when our eyes behold Thy word,
We read Thy Name in fairer lines.

This is poetically expressed, but it is sober truth that
the real character and purpose of God come home to us
far better through the reading of the Bible than through
the wonders of nature. So the reality of God and his
saving power reach us by means of the worship and
fellowship of the church, by the word of God, and by
prayer, and by these means more effectively than by
any others. That is why we speak of these in particular
as *the means of grace*. These are the proven ways by
which the life of the believer is built up and nourished.

1. WHY WE NEED SPECIAL MEANS

You may have heard someone object that it is a sign
of weakness on our part that we have to rely in this way
on a special book and on special routines of religious
observance. They say that every meal ought to be a
sacrament, that we should be able to worship not only
in church but at home or in the office or outdoors, that
any good book should speak to us of God, that we
should be able to see the work of God in the daily news,
that every gathering of friends should be just as holy,
as sacramental, as a church service.

They are quite right. It *is* a sign of weakness. If we
were like the angels in heaven, our every act would be
an expression of praise and love for God and every
moment would be filled with worship.

But we are not angels. We are men and women. We
are sinners. Our lives are not all that we know they

should be. We would like our every word and act to be an expression of our highest ideals, but know they are not. Our sense of duty and of love needs to be pumped up at times. We have to force ourselves to do things we would like to do spontaneously.

We have to teach our children to be polite, put them through the motions of good behaviour, in the hope that some day they will do these things naturally. The means of grace are like that. We ought to be living in constant fellowship with God, but we are not. So it is necessary for us to join in worship in church in order to renew our sense of God's reality, to read the Bible to sustain our sense of his activity in the world, to observe the rites of baptism and communion to assure us of his call, his covenant, his forgiveness, and his transforming power.

If we were perfect we would not require these things. In the heavenly city, we are told, there will be no temple because the Lord God is there (Rev. 21: 22). But we have not yet arrived at that state. So we have as Paul Tillich says, "a Temple beside a town hall, a Lord's Supper beside a daily supper, prayer beside work, meditation beside research." *

2. THE BIBLE AS A MEANS OF GRACE

Protestants have always regarded the Bible as chief among the means of grace. Baptism, the Lord's Supper, preaching, congregational worship, family worship, private devotion — these things have always been thought of as dependent on the Bible. It provides the language for our prayers, our sermons, and even our

---

*The Protestant Era, University of Chicago Press.

hymns. It tells us in words what the sacraments give us in actions. It is a book, but it is a unique book, because it is about unique events and unique persons. In other books you may also read wise and stirring words about God, but no other book can take the place of the Bible in the life of the church. It is through the events and the people of the Bible that God has brought the church into being. It is through understanding these events and especially the event of Christ that we come to understand ourselves as Christians.

If you read a history of Canada you come to understand as a Canadian. All kinds of things you never noticed before begin to seem important. You learn how the early colonists came up the St. Lawrence and how the prairie settlements were dependent on the building of railroads. You begin to see yourself in the picture of a country's growth and history, and realize how the achievement and sacrifice of people in the past help to make you what you are.

If you read the Bible as a book about yourself and not just about people in the past, the same thing happens. *You begin to see yourself in the picture of God's purpose and to understand your own place in it.*

How this happens can be seen in the experience of J. G. Hamann. He spent the spring of 1758 in London reading the Bible to try to shake off his despondency and gloom.

As he read and reflected, he came to feel that the Bible story was the story of his own life, his own neglect of God. In his journal he wrote:

> I recognized my own crimes in the history of the
> Jewish people. I read the course of my own life,

and thanked God for his longsuffering with this
people, since nothing but such an example could
justify me in a like hope.*

One day as he was reading the story of the giving
of the ten commandments he fell into deep meditation.
He thought of Abel, slain by his brother, and felt that
the guilt of Cain was in a sense his own guilt. He
thought of the Son of God slain, and he felt that he
shared somehow in the responsibility for the death of
Christ. He recorded in his journal:

> The Spirit of God went on, in spite of my great
> weakness, and the long resistance I had made . . .,
> to reveal to me more and more the mystery of the
> divine love and the benefit of faith in our gracious
> and only Saviour.†

What happened to Hamann has happened to count-
less Christians. They have read themselves into the
Bible, discovered that its stories were about them, with
their sins and repentances, their aspirations and en-
couragements. They have made themselves characters
in the Bible story, not just in the sense of re-living the
past, but of continuing the biblical past into the present
in their own lives. *What we have to do as Bible readers
is not just learn about the past but make this history
our history.*

This is true for preaching also. Why does the Protestant preacher have a Bible placed before him in the
pulpit? Why does he preach from a biblical text? Why
are passages from the Bible read in the church service?
Not because there aren't other books that are eloquent

---

*J. G. *Hamann* (1730-1788), Ronald Gregor Smith, Collins.
†*Ibid.*

and wise and instructive and inspired, but because this book alone is the source of all we know about Christ and his people. If we want to number ourselves with his people, this book and no other is the one that we must make our own.

3. THE SACRAMENTS AS MEANS OF GRACE

Most of the business of our lives is carried out in words. When we want to tell people things we call them on the telephone or write them letters. In a country where no one speaks your language you are soon overwhelmed with a sense of isolation. When an infant wakes crying in the night, half the frustration for both child and mother comes from the child's inability to *say* what is wrong. The word is the chief means of communication, just as the word of God is the chief means of grace.

Actions, as well as words can speak. Sometimes they speak louder than words. The boy squeezes his girl's hand. Two businessmen shake hands on a deal. These are outward signs which confirm what has been said.

Calvin said the sacraments of the gospel are like that. Baptism and the Lord's Supper don't add anything to what we read in the Bible. But they are God's pledge that it is operative, and are intended to increase and strengthen our faith in the word of God.

Many things can be sacramental in a general way: they express the inward and spiritual by the outward and material. The ritual at a wedding, the laying on of hands in blessing, a curtsey before a queen, these are common examples. Christianity is often said to be a sacramental religion because it takes material things so seriously as expressions of spiritual meaning. It even claims that God himself took flesh upon him in the incarnation to express and act out his spiritual purposes for men. Some have even spoken of the whole universe as being sacramental because every material thing can show us the grandeur of God.

This however is too general. Taken so broadly the meaning of sacrament is too easily lost. But in the stricter meaning of the word only two things are properly called sacraments of the gospel. They alone are solemn rituals or ceremonies directly instituted by Christ himself: baptism and the Lord's Supper. Other rites such as confirmation, ordination, and marriage, have been counted as sacraments by some branches of the church, notably the Roman Catholics. But Protestants reserve the name sacrament for the two which have clear authority from scripture.

Baptists often prefer the term ordinances to sacraments, but hold essentially the same doctrine about them as other Protestants. It was an eminent Baptist, H. Wheeler Robinson, who wrote:

> The two great Sacraments of baptism and the Lord's Supper are the points at which the scattered rays of her (the church's) religious life are brought to a focus. . . . There is always a peril, in any discussion of the Sacraments, that we should allow the examination . . . of different interpretations to obscure the far greater agreement in all that the Sacraments represent.*

4. BAPTISM

> Baptism . . . is the sacrament by which are signed and sealed our union to Christ and participation in the blessings of the new covenant.†

The Christian Experience of the Holy Spirit, Harper & Brothers.
†*The Basis of Union* of The United Church of Canada.

It is the sacrament of entry into the church, into the fellowship of Christ's people.

The element used in baptism is water, and the person being baptized is either sprinkled with it or dipped in it. The symbolism is two-fold: washing from sin (1 Peter 3: 21), and death and rebirth. The washing is obvious in sprinkling; the death and rebirth is fully seen only in immersion where the person baptized is lowered under the water and raised again as though he were being buried and raised up to newness of life (Rom. 6: 4; Col. 2: 12). Although dipping is unusual in many denominations because it is inconvenient, especially with children, it is normally permissible.

We believe that baptism is given us by God as the pledge of his faithfulness. In the covenant which he made with men in Jesus Christ he committed himself to be faithful in all his dealings with them, to forgive their sins if they repent, and to withhold no good gift of his grace. Baptism is God's signature and seal on his covenant. On our side, it is the sign and pledge that we seek the blessings of this covenant and commit ourselves to living faithfully within it. Both God and man have their parts to play in baptism, but God's part comes first. It is he who made the covenant and formed the church. It is he who calls men into the church. Our part is to answer, to follow and to keep faith.

This is well shown in the famous story of Martin Luther who, when he felt himself to be tempted by the devil, chalked on the table before him the words, "I have been baptized." In his moment of weakness, when he doubted whether he had the strength to stand fast, he reminded himself that at his baptism God had given a pledge to him.

One of the great controversies among Protestants is on whether it is proper to baptize infants. The great majority of Christians in all ages answer yes. Baptist churches and some others say no. They argue that an infant cannot have faith, repent of its sins, or commit itself to God, and point out that there is no absolutely certain case in the New Testament of children being baptized. There are many things in the New Testament however that imply infant baptism. In Acts 16: 15 and 33 believers are baptized with all their household or all their family. In Matthew 19: 14, Jesus blessed little children and blamed those who would have kept them from him. And Acts 2: 39, states that the promises of the gospel, like the covenant in the Old Testament, are not only to us, but also to our children.

Admittedly, infant baptism could be abused. If parents do not know what they are doing, or if the church grants it without teaching the solemn undertakings it involves, the sacrament is dishonoured. Not only the parents but also the congregation should be aware that they are obligated to make provision for the Christian nurture of the baptized child. When a good thing is abused we ought not to abolish it but try to use it rightly.

Protestant churches do not teach that baptism is necessary to salvation or that children who die unbaptized are thereby separated from the mercies of God. God gives us baptism to confirm and strengthen us in the faith and as a visible sign and seal of his grace. To refuse it is to neglect the gift and ordinance of God, but the lack of baptism does not bar anyone from God's love and grace.

5. THE LORD'S SUPPER

In its simplest form the Lord's Supper is a fellowship meal of bread and wine in which Christ's people gather with him around a common table. A meal is a common and natural way of expressing fellowship. When we have a guest in our own home we like to show our friendship for him by having him join us at the table. To do so establishes a bond between us. A church supper does the same thing, and we ought to remember that Holy Communion is *the* church supper.

Communion: We know that Jesus was in the habit of eating with his disciples and that on special occasions they had solemn fellowship meals together. The Last Supper in the upper room was such a meal. Jesus knowing, as John says, that his hour was come to depart out of this world, was specially anxious to speak to his disciples about their continuing fellowship with one another and with him (John 13: 1). He asked them to continue this fellowship meal of bread and wine in remembrance of him (1 Cor. 11: 24 ff.) so that they might know that their fellowship with one another and with him would not end with his death. As they gathered around the common table they would know he was still present with them. And this supper was appointed as an outward and visible sign of his presence.

Every time the Lord's Supper is observed in the church we have to think of the fellowship past, present, and future. We are reminded of the fellowship Christ had with his disciples in the days of his flesh. We rejoice in the fellowship that we have with him now, for he is not a dead and buried teacher but a risen and a present Saviour. But we also look forward into the future, and the communion we hope to have with him in the life to come.

Thanksgiving: There are many names for the Lord's Supper. One of them we have already seen: the Holy Communion. Another is the Mass, a term used by Roman Catholics. Yet another is the Divine Liturgy or Divine Service, a term used by Eastern Orthodox churches. One which is specially important, and which we ought perhaps to use more frequently, is the Eucharist. It comes from the Greek word for 'thanksgiving', and reminds us that Christ gave thanks at the supper in the upper room, and that the supper ought to be for us first and foremost an act of thanksgiving.

Many communion services suggest mourning and gloom rather than thanksgiving. They give the impression that the cross and passion were nothing more than a tragedy, that we are commemorating a lost leader rather than rejoicing in the fellowship of a living Lord. The normal time to celebrate the sacrament is not Friday afternoon when he was crucified or even Thursday evening when he instituted the supper, but Sunday morning when he rose triumphant and turned his people from dismay to joy.

Here again past, present, and future are mingled. At the Eucharist we renew the thanksgiving of the first Christians. We join ourselves with the thanksgiving of the whole church in all the world and with the heavenly host when, "with angels and archangels and with all the company of heaven, we laud and magnify" God's glorious name.

In the communion we commemorate and give thanks
for what God has done for us. We are not just commemorating the Last Supper, nor even the cross, but
the whole triumph of God in Christ in his life and
passion, his death and resurrection, his ascension and
his rule at God's right hand.

Sacrifice: The Lord's Supper is concerned also with
sacrifice. Jesus himself said, "This is my body . . . this
is my blood," connecting the bread and wine with his
sacrifice on the cross. The prayer of consecration in
the communion service reminds us that Jesus made on
the cross a full, perfect and sufficient sacrifice for the
sins of the whole world. In it we plead before God
his eternal sacrifice, and make in response our own
sacrifice of praise and thanksgiving, and also the offering of ourselves, our souls and bodies, in God's service.

Sacrifice has always been a part of religion. In Old
Testament times there was an elaborate system of
sacrifice for the forgiveness of sins. The early Christians
came to believe, and the Letter to the Hebrews teaches
in some detail, that this long history of sacrifice had
now come to a climax in Christ. He offered himself
as the perfect and complete sacrifice which was sufficient for the washing away of the sins of the whole
world.

If we no longer have to offer sacrifices on an altar it
is because there is nothing more that needs to be added
or can be added to what Christ has done. The Lord's
Supper itself does not add anything to the sacrifice
of Christ. Rather it "pleads" it. When we come before
God we rest our case, so to speak, on what Christ has
done for us. And God, for his part, has given us the
sacrament as a sign and seal of the fact that he has

accepted Christ's sacrifice and applies it to us. What is required of us now is not that we should try to repeat Christ's sacrifice or add anything to it as though it were insufficient, but gladly accept it and go on to live our lives by its power.

Paul wrote (Rom. 12: 1) that we should offer ourselves as living sacrifices and that this is to be our spiritual worship. Paul seems to be comparing what sacrifice meant before Christ with what it should mean to a Christian. The old sacrifice was material; the Christian sacrifice is spiritual. In the old system men offered an animal for slaughter, but we are to offer our lives to be lived for God.

Remembering these things we should not hesitate to partake of Holy Communion because we feel unworthy of it. Of course we are unworthy of it, as we are unworthy of the sacrifice of Christ. If we were worthy we would not need it. It was for sinners that Christ died and it is sinners that are summoned to the table. We do not come "trusting in our own righteousness, but in God's manifold and great mercies." We are not worthy so much as to gather up the crumbs under the table. When Paul warned against eating and drinking in an unworthy manner (1 Cor. 11: 27 ff.) he was thinking of those who might come thoughtlessly and irreverently, without a due consideration of their need and the wonder of God's love for us shown in this sacrament.

6. COMMON WORSHIP

Worship is the most widely used means of grace among Christians. In this of course the Bible and the sacraments have a large place, as does prayer. But the worship of the Christian fellowship has a distinctive quality and importance that make it worth while thinking about by itself.

At the same time it is noteworthy that Christian worship is extremely varied. On the one hand there is Quaker worship which has no sacraments and no set forms and may consist mainly of the meeting sitting in silent meditation, broken only when some member feels led by the Spirit to speak. On the other there is the Roman mass, an elaborate ritual in Latin with every word and gesture fixed and formalized, a service performed by the priest with or without a congregation, and at which worshippers appear to be only spectators.

In spite of its variety Christian worship in all its forms has a common base. The Christian fellowship gathers in one place, draws apart from the traffic of daily life, and comes into the presence of the living God, the God who speaks, the God who saves. They come to listen to him and to open their souls to his grace.

Habit and custom have a lot to do with the forms of worship, and they have a lot to do with the behaviour of the worshippers. This is not a bad thing, for while there are times in the experience of all of us when our worship does not seem to bring God into our lives, the habit carries us through the period of 'dryness' to a time when he comes with fresh power, and we realize that all the while he has been working in our souls, unseen and unfelt.

Beneath the forms, deeper than the customs by which we seek to practise our religion, is the attitude of the worshipper. E. F. Scott points out that the writers of the Gospels lay down the principles that should govern worship. "No formal directions are given," he says. "All the emphasis is laid on the inner meaning of each act of worship, and the frame of mind in which it should be performed."* The importance of the attitude of the worshipper is summed up thus by William Temple:

> To worship is to quicken the conscience by the holiness of God, to feed the mind with the truth of God, to purge the imagination by the beauty of God, to open the heart to the love of God, to devote the will to the purpose of God. All this is gathered up in that emotion which most cleanses us from selfishness because it is the most selfless of all emotions—adoration.†

So the various means of grace are all part of a spiritual discipline by which the central convictions of the Christian faith are spelled out and acted out. By them we come to a deeper understanding of what God is saying to us and seeking to do for us. And through them, as we respond in faith, his saving power flows into our lives.

The Purpose of the Gospels, Charles Scribner's Sons.
†*The Hope of a New World*, SCM Press Ltd.

Chapter 17

The Church and the World

*To bear its witness to God in the world
the church must educate. It must
work for social welfare and reform.
Being in the world and not of it
the church should be independent of the
state. A world church is emerging.*

What is the church for? If you were to judge by some of the things you see you might be pardoned for thinking that the church exists to keep Christians happy, to provide a warm and secure society, to protect them from the world outside, and to get them into heaven when they die. If this is the impression the church gives, then something has gone wrong. You have only to reflect a moment to realize that the church does not exist for its own sake. It was founded in order to do God's will. It exists to serve the world, not itself.

"Go therefore and make disciples of all nations," said the risen Lord, "and you shall be my wit-

nesses in Jerusalem and in all Judea and Samaria
and to the end of the earth" (Matt. 28: 19; Acts
1: 8).

A primary task of the church is to be a witness for
God and bear testimony to what he is, what he has
done and what he is still doing. But how can you be a
witness? Two things are needed: you must learn to
speak so that you can be understood, and you must
show by your actions what you mean.

1. The church and education

I once heard of a group of missionaries who went out
to China to preach the gospel. They went around the
villages preaching in English, and when they got no
response passed on to the next village shaking the dust
off their feet in accordance with Matthew 10: 14. One
would like to think that the story is untrue. Unfortunately we all tend to act like this to some degree.
Everyone would agree that these missionaries were
hopelessly and ludicrously in the wrong. They spoke
a language no one could understand, and their actions
did nothing to express the message they were trying to
communicate.

What *should* they have done? First they should
have learned Chinese. Then they would have to find
ways to express in Chinese what they had to say. It
takes a long time to put over new ideas to a child even
in one's own language. How much more difficult when
you have to teach in a foreign tongue that may not have
words to express what you want to say.

When the first Christians went out to convert people
who spoke Greek or Latin, they had to face the same
problems. They had to translate from one language

into another, and they had to educate people in the meaning of new ideas, for people brought up on the Greek religions would think very differently about God from people brought up on the Old Testament.

Christianity is after all an educated religion. If the church is to do its job people must be trained to read the Bible, to translate it from Greek and Hebrew into other languages, to explain it and defend it, to compare it with other religions and ways of life. At the time of Christ the Jews had long been an educated people— and among them education was for all the members of the religious community. So it is in the Christian church. Wherever it spread it founded schools to train preachers and some of these quickly grew into great institutions of higher learning. But more than that, every congregation became a kind of school where every Christian was taught to read the Bible and understand the meaning of Christian faith and the duties of Christian life.

This still happens on the mission fields, for how can the church do its work among ignorant and superstitious people without educating them? Even if you begin with a most narrow and other-worldly view of what it means to "preach the gospel" you are almost at once involved in literacy campaigns, church schools, Bible schools, translating and printing the scriptures and Christian literature, running theological colleges, and so on. All over the world the Christian church has been a great educational force.

This is true not only for India and Africa which we still think of as mission fields, but for Europe, which once was barbarian and where almost all the old schools and universities were founded by the church.

It is true also in North America. The Puritans who settled Massachusetts and founded Harvard University said this about it:

> After God had carried us safe to New England . . . and we had rear'd convenient places for worship; one of the next things we looked after was to advance Learning . . . dreading to leave an illiterate ministry, when our present ministers shall lie in the dust.

The same thing could be said about many of our Canadian universities. The church needs an educational system to do its own proper work, and it will always have to find ways and means of getting one. Thus the church is inescapably involved with the world, and in particular with the world of learning.

One of the best illustrations of this is in the monastic movement. The early monks were Christians who were anxious to flee from the world, live a life of rigorous discipline, and save their own souls. The last thing they were concerned about was the social witness of the church and the transformation of society. Yet the monasteries became the church's most powerful weapon both in missionary work and in social work. The monks built up schools and libraries, cared for the young and the sick, set up hospices and rest-houses for travellers and the aged. All of which proves that once you start to be a Christian anything can happen, for God may lead you to results far different from what you expected.

2. THE CHURCH AND THE SOCIAL ORDER

Most missionary movements begin not as attempts to build up a Christian civilization or to reform pagan cultures, but as attempts to preach the gospel and save people's souls. They begin with a very simple message, "Repent and be baptized," and a very simple task, to get people converted. Often the greatest missionary efforts have been urged on by the thought that the world is coming to an end and there isn't much time left. Some people may think these are crude and narrow interpretations of Christianity, but they embody important truths: that *conversion is central* and that *the task is urgent.*

To get things moving you have to concentrate on essentials and that is what Christian pioneers have always done when they are moving into a new land. They travel light, and the institutions of a Christian civilization are built up only by the second and third generations. But they must be built up. Just as you can't preach the gospel without building up an educational system, so *you can't preach the gospel without being concerned for social welfare.* Why have Christian missionaries started hospitals as well as schools wherever they have gone? Because the gospel they go to proclaim is all about the love of God for man, and anyone who believes it must act that way. "Beloved, if God so loved us, we also ought to love one another" (1 John 4: 11). Who would believe in a gospel of love that did not lead people to love one another? How will people know what a gospel of love means unless they see it in action?

> To be a witness you must learn to speak so that you can be understood: that is why the church has to be involved in education. To be a witness you have also to show what you mean by your actions: that is why the church is always involved in social work.

Social work does not only mean setting up social agencies; it also means social reform. When the Christian church moves into a non-Christian culture it usually finds itself opposed to some of the things it finds there, things such as slavery, the subjugation of women, the opium traffic, and the buying and selling of wives.

The church is, or ought to be, a reforming force. Even where a civilization has been under Christian influence for centuries there is reforming left to be done. Situations change and demand new action and new attitudes. The industrial revolution for instance required a complete rethinking of traditional Christian ideas with regard to things like trade unions, child labour laws, interest rates, and property rights. And the process of rethinking is often a painful one.

The Old Testament lays down rules for right human relations which express the conviction that God is the protector of the poor and expects us to be the same. For instance, it teaches fields are not to be gleaned by the owner at harvest time, but the fallen grain and that in the fence rows must be left to be gathered by the needy (Lev. 23: 22). But how relevant is this in an age of combine harvesters, grain elevators, government subsidies, and large cities thousands of miles from the wheat fields?

The principle holds good, the poor must be protected, but new methods must be found, and in a complex society it may take many experts a long time to find the right means and a longer time to persuade the church and the nation to adopt them. And since times seem always to be changing the process of reform never ends.

Christians are not necessarily more expert in politics and economics than other people, and the pronouncements of church committees often turn out to be woefully inadequate, but Christians are expected to be morally alert, sensitive to injustice, and concerned about righteousness not only in their personal lives but in society. That is why Christians ought always to be reformers, though not of course hasty and unwise ones.

Unfortunately Christians and the church itself often get on the wrong side of social issues. In the struggle against slavery in the nineteenth century there were many Christians who defended slavery with might and main. There are Christians today who support racial segregation and inequality. Why do these things happen? First because Christians can be sinful, stupid and, like everyone else, ignorant. Also because times change, issues are complex and the teaching of the Bible and tradition cannot be directly applied.

Take *the case of slavery.* The New Testament does not preach abolition but urges slaves to serve their masters willingly (Col. 3: 22; 1 Cor. 7: 20-24) and masters to treat their slaves well (Col. 4: 1) since "in Christ" the distinction between a slave and a master no longer applies (Gal. 3: 28).

It was easy for slave owners to believe that the New Testament approved of slavery. Were they right? Why does the New Testament not urge the abolition of slavery? First, because in New Testament times it was not possible to abolish slavery. The early Christians would have been glad if it were, for many of them were slaves. But when few if any Christians had any

political power or influence there was little they could
do directly. Only when Christians began to have a
share of power did the situation begin to change. One
of the first things that the Emperor Constantine did
after he became a Christian was to make it easier for
slaves to gain their freedom, forbid the splitting up of
slave families when estates were sold and forbid brand-
ing on the face because "the face is fashioned after the
likeness of the heavenly beauty."

In the long run it is fair to say that slavery was
brought to an end by the Christian conscience. The
church has much to be ashamed of in her social record,
but much more for which to be thankful and to praise
God.

3. IN THE WORLD BUT NOT OF IT

One of the most interesting things about the church
is the way it always seems to live in some kind of
tension with the world, sometimes at peace, sometimes
at war, usually a little awkward and unpredictable to
the politicians. It is *in* the world, real enough as a
social group or a political factor, but never quite *of*
the world so that its behaviour can never be charted
and predicted like that of political groups. It has a life
of its own and mysterious sources of vitality that have
kept it going over the centuries, though humanly speaking it ought to have died out long ago. It is capable of
being reborn and re-energised when it seems weakest.
This unpredictability is just what you would expect
if the church really is a divine institution and not a
human one. It is fascinating to see the twists and turns
of church life over the centuries, and you can see the

hand of God in the history of the church just as surely as in the history of the old Israel.

To begin with, the church was an insignificant group of heretical Jews in process of breaking away from the Old Israel, and yet convinced that they were really the new and true Israel. They had no wealth, no power, no learning worth speaking of. Not many wise, not many powerful, not many noble were called, said Paul. It was among slaves and the poor and outcast of the city that the church grew fastest. But it showed power: it transformed people's lives, it gave the hopeless a hope and the worthless a dignity. Within three centuries of the death of Christ it had spread all over the known world, had produced schools and scholars, an impressive literature, a system of doctrine, a strong way of life, and a disciplined body of believers who stood out in an uncertain and decaying world as a people with a purpose.

No wonder they began to attract converts among the mighty. It was perhaps inevitable that in the end the Roman Emperor himself should become a convert. Several of the emperors, suspicious of the influence of the young church, had tried to suppress it by persecution, but persecution only seemed to make it stronger. Finally, the Emperor Constantine accepted Christ.

The reversal of fortunes was sudden. When in 325 Constantine summoned the famous council of bishops of Nicaea many of those who came and were entertained with imperial splendour had been tortured and imprisoned in the persecutions. Christians hardly knew what to make of it. Some of them thought the kingdom of God was come at last, and when Constantine built his great cathedral in his new capital city of Constantinople, one bishop preached a sermon on Revelation 21: 2 and said the new Jerusalem was coming down from heaven. Yet others were suspicious and thought that it was a plot on the devil's part to entangle the church in the snares of the world and rob her of her strength.

When they saw hundreds and thousands of converts seeking entry into the fold, some regarded it as a God-given opportunity for social reform and moral leadership, and much good was done along these lines. But others feared the church was becoming infected by pagan ways, and turned to monasticism and a strictly disciplined life in order to protect the church's integrity. Much good came from that, too. Apart from the individual souls that may have been saved the monasteries became great centres of devotion and learning, evangelism and social service.

When a century or so later the Roman Empire finally began to fall apart and become a prey to barbarian invasions, many of the old-fashioned pagans blamed the catastrophe on the corrosive influence of Christianity. But the church was the only strong force left. And men turned to it as the natural guardian of justice and civilized virtue.

So it was that all through the Dark Ages in Europe, between the fifth and the tenth centuries, men turned to the church as the source and safeguard of culture. We call those ages "dark" because they were times of political disorder and unrest, but they were also times of great missionary expansion into the pagan lands of North Europe: France, Germany, Scandinavia, and Great Britain; and when a great civilization rose again in Europe in the Middle Ages complete with great cathedrals and universities it was on Christian foundations that it was built.

If Protestants wonder why the Roman church acts the way it does in Spain or Quebec or South America, seeking to control education and social and political life either directly or by laying down the principles that politicians are to put into practice, they should remember that it still tends to think of the Middle Ages as the ideal situation for the church. In those days almost all educated men were clerics, who because of this education controlled the universities, the schools, and the civil service. The church naturally took the lead because there was no one else to do it. They put the policies of the church into operation because that was what they believed in. And mediaeval Christian civilization in Europe was an immensely impressive achievement.

It was very different of course from the situation of Paul's little congregation in Corinth. Now *all* the wise, the powerful, and the noble were called, and if you weren't a Christian and a member of the church in good standing you had small chance of success in this world, to say nothing of the next. All through the Middle Ages there were sincere Christians who wondered if this was really good for the church. Monasticism continued to flourish as a protest against worldliness, but even monastic orders can grow rich and powerful and worldly, and many did. By the end of the Middle Ages many of the best Christians began to wonder if it would not be better for the church to lose her power and wealth and prestige in this world in order that she might again become rich towards God.

Some even began to advocate what we call *the separation of church and state.*

It would be a mistake to say that this was the line that the Protestants took at the Reformation. All the great reformers of the first generation of Protestantism: Luther, Calvin, and Cranmer, for instance, believed in established churches and the persecution of heretics, and did not believe in religious toleration. It was only the smaller movements such as the Anabaptists that took this radical line, so different from that of the Middle Ages. Sometimes they took it because, being minority groups, they had no hope or expectation of ever being established themselves as official churches in any land.

Since the end of the seventeenth century, however, the position most widely accepted among Protestants is that it is better for the church to be independent of the state. There are even signs that the Roman church also is moving this way. When there is separation between church and state, the church becomes, as far as the state is concerned, a voluntary society which no one is compelled to join and no one is penalized for not joining. The church, on its part, seeks to influence public morality and political policy only by those methods which are available to other citizens, and recognizes the right of non-Christians to take the same part in political life that Christians do. The church, no longer protected by special privilege, has to take part in free and open debate and believes that this will help to stimulate it to new obedience and greater awareness of the changing needs of the world. Like the church of the early centuries it has to live by its spiritual vitality and not by its earthly power.

4. THE COMING OF THE WORLD CHURCH

There is another new factor which enters into church-state relations today. From the time of Constantine till the end of the nineteenth century the church was largely European, including European colonies overseas. European civilization could safely be called Christian. There were of course churches outside the European areas, but they tended to be tiny minorities, or colonial churches, or missions. Europe could be called Christian just as India could be called Hindu and Middle East Muslim. The world was divided into well-marked religious and cultural regions.

This is no longer true. The success of the great missionary movements of the last century and a half has meant that the church is now strong in many places outside the old "Christendom". We can no longer think of the churches in India and Africa as missions, but think of them rather as "younger churches." In many ways the younger churches are more creative and faster growing than the old ones. And *for almost the first time in history we have to think in terms of a world church.* The church has always been in principle a world church ("go ye into all the world"), but in practice it was mainly a European church because that was where its dominant strength lay. But now it looks as if the church is becoming genuinely international and intercultural for the first time. The ecumenical movement is one of the signs of this. It is not just a movement to unite old European denominations. It has become in fact a world church movement and many people think of it as the beginning of a new stage in church history.

Chapter 18

The Kingdom of God

Jesus' teaching about the kingdom of God has not been lost. As light passing through a prism is split into bands of colour, it is seen in our faith about the church, heaven, and the goal of history, and in Christ himself.

People often say that Jesus of Nazareth has been betrayed by the Christian church. He was a simple man, they say, who came with a simple message about loving God and loving your neighbour, but the church has messed it up with a lot of theology nobody can understand. They say he was a poor man who came to poor people, but the church has become rich, powerful and worldly. And they say much more. Many of these charges are false and the people who make them just don't understand. Still there is an uncomfortable amount of truth in some of them.

1. WHAT HAPPENED TO THE GOOD NEWS OF THE
   KINGDOM

Take this, for instance: The kingdom of God is the
central theme in the teaching of Jesus, but there has
been precious little about the kingdom in the official
teaching of the church. In the Gospels Jesus is always
talking about the kingdom. His very first sermon, so
Mark tells us, was, "The kingdom of God is at hand."
Practically all his parables are about the kingdom. Yet
the teachings of the early church hardly mention it.
The word "kingdom" doesn't even appear in the index
to the standard work on the teaching of the church
in the first five centuries.* The early church argued
about baptism, about whether to have bishops, about
what sins could or could not be forgiven, about the
Trinity, about the divinity of Christ, but hardly ever
did they talk about the kingdom. When they did it
was usually to say that the kingdom was more or less
the same thing as the church.

A standard textbook of Roman Catholic theology
still takes very much this view. The only qualification
it makes is to say in a footnote,

> We may note, for it is sometimes overlooked, that
> theologians do not identify *tout court* the Catholic
> Church with the Kingdom of God. The Church is
> the Kingdom of God *on earth.*†

Protestant text books have a little more to say about
the kingdom. They speak of establishing the kingdom
of God at the end of history, and about heaven, as do

---

*J. N. D. Kelly: *Early Christian Doctrines*, A. & C. Black.
†G. D. Smith, ed.: *The Teaching of the Catholic Church*, Burns &
Oates.

the Roman Catholics. But the kingdom certainly does not seem to have the central place in the teaching of any church that it seems to have had in the teaching of Jesus. That looks bad. Is it as bad as it looks? Why did it happen?

For one thing, Christians very early came to the conclusion that Jesus must have been misunderstood about the kingdom. He seemed to be saying that the kingdom was coming very soon and was practically here:

> Mark 1: 15—"the kingdom of God is at hand. . . ."
>
> Mark 9: 1—"there are some standing here who will not taste death before they see the kingdom of God come with power."
>
> Mark 13: 30—"this generation will not pass away before all these things take place."

Paul wrote to the Thessalonians as if he expected to live to see the return of the Lord and the establishment of the kingdom: "We who are alive, who are left until the coming of the Lord" (1 Thess. 4: 15). But the years passed and nothing happened. Paul began to doubt whether he would see the establishment of the kingdom before his death (Phil. 1: 20 ff.).

He did die and the kingdom had not come.

The church remembered that Jesus had said (Acts 1: 7), "It is not for you to know the times or seasons," and "of that day and hour no one knows, not even the angels of heaven, nor the Son, but the Father only"

(Matt. 24: 36; Mark 13: 32). And so they all settled down to wait.

Some wait! If you think this was the time that Christianity began to slow down to a walk you are very wrong. This was the very time when the young church was growing all over the Roman empire, gaining converts, withstanding persecution, transforming the lives of individuals and of families, laying the foundations of the Christian world. It was a pretty powerful kind of waiting, a waiting upon God that was combined with the most active service of God. I often think *this was the real testing time of the church.*

The church never seems to have faltered, but it did change. Part of that change was the new way in which it began to think about the kingdom. The early church did not *forget* Jesus' teaching. It did not abandon it just because the kingdom was not coming in the expected way. It did begin to rethink the whole business in a new way and in the light of its new experience.

You know what happens when clear sunlight passes through a glass prism—it splits up into reds and yellows and blues, a whole rainbow of colours appears out of what was plain white light. It seems to me that something like that happened to Jesus' teaching about the kingdom. When it had passed through the experience of the young church the teaching about the kingdom, which in the mouth of Jesus had been as clear and direct and single as the sunlight, broke into different and separated teachings about the church, about heaven, and about the goal of history.

2. THE KINGDOM AND THE CHURCH

The early church was not wrong, and the Roman church today is not wrong, in connecting the church with the kingdom. Jesus said that he had come to bring the kingdom and as they looked back they saw that the major result of Jesus' life and ministry had been the establishing of the church. What was the church but a fellowship of people who acknowledged God as King, tried to live as dutiful subjects, fought the King's battles, and felt themselves to be empowered by his Spirit?

What more natural than to think of the church as the spiritual kingdom which Jesus came to found? What more natural than to think that as the church grew and pressed on with its missionary task the kingdom of God was being established on earth like a great empire, and the kingdoms of this world were becoming the kingdom of the Lord, and that this should go on till

> Jesus shall reign where'er the sun
> Does his successive journeys run,
> His Kingdom stretch from shore to shore. . . .

The early church must have seen all this in a quite vivid and thrilling way. As the old Roman Empire began to wheeze and creak and stagger to its collapse the young church began to take it over in the name of God. When the Emperor Constantine himself became a Christian and founded a new capital with a magnificent Christian church in the middle of it, one sober Christian leader described it all as if the kingdom had now finally come in its completeness. He compared the new Christian capital which the emperor had built to the new Jerusalem come down from heaven which was prophesied in the book of Revelation.

This was around A.D. 330. Think of what has happened since! Wars, calamities, corruption of the church, defeats that justice and mercy have suffered. We may wonder that anybody could be so simple-minded as to suppose that the kingdom had come then. But you can see why he thought it.

As the church began to gather to itself more and more political power the popes at Rome became the most powerful rulers in the western world. The feeling grew that the kingly rule of God and the earthly power of the church were much the same thing. To this day the Roman church seems to think largely in these terms. And Roman Catholics are very serious and high-minded about it. It is no mere lust for power. It is a serious conviction that the church bears the kingdom with it and that the power and influence of the church grows so the kingdom comes in its fulness.

What should a Protestant say to this? He should say that the church is *indeed* a divine institution. It is *indeed* the task of the church to work for the establishment of the kingdom. The transformation of the world by the influence of Christianity is *indeed* one of the ways in which the kingdom comes. But it must also be said that the church is made up of sinful and fallible men, and they do not necessarily become any less sinful and fallible when they gain great power. God will use the church as he used the nation Israel to advance his purposes and establish his rule, but the church can go wrong, as Israel went wrong. And God can punish the church as he punished Israel.

The church has no monopoly on God. He can work without it if he wants to. God works his will and builds his kingdom among the heathen and the outsiders while we are sleeping in our pews. And when we wake up it will be to the shame and disgrace of finding that God has been fighting his own battles and we haven't even been there.

How much is the church doing about the race problem? How much are we doing about poverty, disease, and injustice in Africa, India? How much are we doing about the underprivileged races in Canada? Won't we be ashamed if it turns out that there have been Muslims and communists and atheists who have done more for the kingdom in these last days than we Christians?

In the parable of the sheep and the goats at the last judgment, the unrighteous who were condemned were indignant because they thought they had been good people who had never failed in their duty to God. And the righteous who were rewarded were equally surprised. They hadn't been thinking about God at all, but only doing the decent thing. Let us be warned. The church *is* the instrument of the kingdom. It *is* its business to work for God. But the sternest judgments are reserved for those who desert the highest posts.

So I say, Christians have not been wrong in connecting the church and the kingdom. The church is the instrument for building the kingdom; it ought to show the first fruits of the kingdom. But let us be careful not to claim that it *is* the kingdom in such a way that we become proud and arrogant and provoke God to cast us out and put another in our place.

3. THE KINGDOM OF HEAVEN

There is a second way in which Jesus' teaching about the kingdom was broken up and refracted, and that is the teaching about heaven. In Matthew's Gospel you rarely see the phrase "the kingdom of God." Usually it is "the kingdom of heaven." It means the same thing. Matthew as a devout Jew did not like to take the name of God too easily on his lips lest he seem to take the name of the Lord in vain, so he usually says heaven instead, just as we often say the Almighty. It is probably only an accident, but this change of words points to a change of thought among the Christians about the kingdom of God. Just as part of Jesus' teaching about the kingdom was applied to the church, so part of it was applied to heaven.

In the book of Revelation, John introduces a vision by saying, "I looked and behold, a door was opened in heaven." He describes how he went through the door and saw the angels and the archangels and God sitting on a throne. It is no good asking *where* heaven is; you won't get a straight answer to that question. Obviously it is the place where God does his ruling, where he sits in his majesty and governs. If the kingdom of God means God's rule and government surely heaven must have some close connection with the kingdom. We know the dangers of this kind of talk. God is not bounded in space. His kingdom and his presence have no boundaries. He is everywhere, so heaven is not any one place. But still we can't help thinking in terms of space so we naturally think of heaven as above the bright blue sky. Everyone does. When we think of God we look up.

In the war we used to talk about people who were blown up as being "blown to kingdom come" as though "kingdom come" were a place you could reach if you went high enough to get into orbit. We smile when we say these things because we know they can't be taken too literally. All the same, a whole system of thought has been built up out of them. It is sometimes called *the three-storey universe: heaven, earth, and hell.* We live our lives on earth and when we die we either go up to heaven or down to hell. Popular Christianity especially before the Reformation imagined it all in great detail and it was very widely and uncritically believed. In its way it is true enough and it does portray important things: for example, God is King now. Whether people on earth see it or not, whether the world looks as though God were ruling or not, he is. And somewhere it is possible to see and to know the reality of his reign.

All that is to the good. But there are very bad things about this three-storey universe view of the kingdom of God. It suggests for instance that God may rule in heaven, but this earth is a kind of no man's land over which he has no more rights than the devil: happily we don't have to live long on earth and when we die we can shake the dust off and go to heaven and leave the world behind. Many people believe that this is Christianity.

But they overlook some very important parts of scripture, for instance:

God so loved the *world* that he gave his only Son . . . (John 3: 16).
For in him all the fulness of God was pleased to

dwell, and through him to reconcile to himself all things, whether on earth or in heaven . . . (Col. 1: 19, 20).

These passages seem to teach that God does not intend to save us *out* of the world but to save us *with* the world. The plan of redemption is not an emergency operation in which God will rescue a few lucky souls from a world that has gone hopelessly wrong and is past God's power to save. The world as a whole is God's creation and his plan of redemption is a plan for it all. He wants not just individuals, snatched up to heaven, but somehow that the world, society, human history, should be redeemed and brought to a victorious climax, in which his will shall be done on earth as it is in heaven, and his kingdom come on earth.

This kind of teaching, which says the kingdom is the same thing as heaven could be called *vertical eschatology*. When you die you go vertically up to heaven or vertically down to hell, and that's that. It is a crude kind of teaching and rather unbiblical. But it is so widespread that it is worth while trying to show what is wrong with it. First, it is too selfish and individualist: lead a good life here for three score years and ten and you will be rewarded with the joys of heaven and escape the punishments of hell. This life is just a kind of test, a probation, by which people's eternal destinies are settled. Human history seems to have no value of its own; it is simply a testing ground for souls. History doesn't have to have any meaning as a whole, it isn't going anywhere.

That is just where this vertical, individual theory

falls short. We feel that not only should our individual lives have meaning, but history as a whole ought to have a meaning. Not only is God *our* Lord, but he is the Lord of history. It is clear that the Bible thinks this way, too. All these difficult ideas in the Bible about the last judgment, the second coming, the resurrection of the body, the millennial kingdom, the new Jerusalem, show that the Bible doesn't think of our story as ending two minutes after we die and find ourselves either in heaven or in hell. Somehow or other we are bound up with history; convinced that God is concerned with us, not only as individuals but as parts of society, of the whole drama of history. Somehow or other we will be there at the end. And maybe our redemption will not be complete until God has worked out the whole of his purposes for all men and all history. You may think it all very speculative, but what does the last judgment and the resurrection of the body mean if it does not mean that our redemption is not a separate thing but is bound up with the redemption of all God's creatures?

"It belongs to the very heart of salvation that we cannot have it in fulness until all for whom it is intended have it together . . . none of us can be made whole unless we are made whole together."*

That does not mean that all men will be saved. I think it means that where any are lost this is a tragedy not only for them, but for all.

---

*Lesslie Newbigin: *The Household of God,* SCM Press Ltd.

4. THE KINGDOM AND THE GOAL OF HISTORY

This vertical, individual view of the kingdom as heaven, where we go when we die, needs to be supplemented by a horizontal view. This will emphasize the fact that God's redemption has to do with the whole of history and not individuals only. The kingdom is not just a place in heaven to which we escape when we die but something being built in history, to be complete only when God brings the story of history to a conclusion. This is the third way of talking about the kingdom.

One expression of this horizontal view is the "social gospel."

A generation ago when it was in full strength the social gospel was a protest against the kind of revivalist religion that made men think too much of their own personal salvation, and allowed them to be indifferent to the social evils around them. It was a call and a challenge to men to forget self and go out and work for the kingdom in this world, that justice might be done and righteousness abound and God's name be honoured. By social reform, through unemployment insurance, better hospitals, universal education, and world peace, the kingdom was to be brought in. It was to be built also by foreign missions. "The evangelization of the world in this generation" was a great crusading slogan of sixty years ago. Men and women went out to build schools and churches and hospitals among the heathen that the kingdom might come.

Much of this is unfashionable today. We *have* our unemployment insurance and our baby bonuses, and

the kingdom hasn't come that much closer to fulfilment. The social gospel with its optimism seems naive
and unrealistic against the reality of sin and evil. But
there is something heart-warming about the social
gospel, something honest and generous and hopeful.

The social gospel did have this weakness, that it
tended to become secular. With its emphasis on work
in the world it sometimes gave the impression that if
you had a properly organized society all our human
problems would disappear, that a world with no war,
no hunger, no disease, and no ignorance, would be the
kingdom, and this is something we are quite able to
bring in if we work hard enough at it. An old teacher
of mine once said to me: "When we were young we
talked about going out to build the kingdom of God.
It was really going to be *our* kingdom because we
were to build it, but it was going to be so good that we
would call it the kingdom of God." The kingdom of
God had been reduced to a human utopia, not very
different in spirit from the kind of classless society and
paradise that the communists are trying to build.

Both those who identify the kingdom with the church
and those who think of the kingdom as the goal of our
history have to be reminded that the kingdom is God's
and not man's, that he reigns on high and that his ways
are not ours to scrutinize. They have to be reminded
that when the kingdom comes it will not necessarily
come to put the seal of approval and the final touch of
perfection on all our schemes for world betterment.
The Bible makes it very clear that the kingdom will
come in judgment as well as in fulfilment, to cast down

as well as to build up. Some of the things to be cast down on the last day will be the empires of the wicked, the communists, and the brewers, and all the other ogres whom we denounce in our church meetings. Other things that will be cast down will include some of the castles we have been building ourselves which turned out to be less innocent than we had hoped.

5. THE KINGDOM REVEALED IN CHRIST

I began by saying that the kingdom was central to the teaching of Jesus, but that in the teaching of the Christian theology it has been fragmented into separate doctrines about the church, about heaven, and about the goal of history. These all have some portion of truth in them. But they need one another. They supplement one another. That is hardly surprising, for our doctrines are always partial and incomplete statements of the truth which need to be supplemented by one another and corrected by one another.

If it is true that God can reveal himself only in a person, and never in a doctrine or a book, all our doctrines are going to have to be called in question by what Jesus himself was and what he did. We may try to say in words what the kingdom is, or we may try to define it in doctrines, but Jesus himself never did. He simply told stories to illustrate what the kingdom was like, and finally showed what it was like by what he did and by what he was. As Origen once said, Jesus was himself the kingdom, the kingdom in person.

How very simple and direct it all is when we meet the kingdom in *person*. You and I haven't trodden the

ways of Galilee or met the Master in the flesh. But if
we have any kind of faith and any real Christianity in
our lives, it is not because of the books we have read
but the people we have met. We have seen the kingdom in action in someone's life.

Jesus was himself the kingdom. Wherever he was
the kingdom was present. Wherever he healed the sick
or bound up the broken heart, there the kingdom was
at work.

> If it is by the finger of God that I cast out demons,
> then the kingdom of God has come upon you
> (Luke 11: 20).
> The kingdom of God is in the midst of you (Luke
> 17: 21).

When he became the friend of publicans and sinners
he was showing the ways of the kingdom of God. When
he who was so naturally the master made himself a
servant, there the kingdom of God was at work. When
he broke through all the stiff rules and conventions of
the religious people of his day in order to help the
distressed and the deserted, the kingdom was there.

This is what must always be our guide and our check
in the Christian life.

If the kingdom was real and present in Jesus and his
works, it should still be real and present in the community which is his body. Jesus lives today, not only
in heaven, but in the Christian church and therefore
the kingdom is present and active today not only in
heaven but in the Christian church, which is bringing
in the kingdom, praying, "Thy kingdom come," in word
and deed.

We are like soldiers in an army of liberation. A landing has been made in an enemy occupied territory. On our D-Day the bridgehead was established. The banners of the kingdom of God were set up again in this world. Now we are between D-Day and V-Day. We know that the decisive victory has been won. We know that final victory is now assured. But there is hard discipline and fighting ahead for us before the war is over. D-Day was when Christ established the bridgehead of the kingdom. V-Day is when the kingdom will be finally triumphant. Our part is in between. We have to press forward, exploit the gains, harass the enemy. The campaign may be bitter and it may be long, but we know that since the Son of God went forth to war the final victory is assured.